W9-AYM-198

THROW AWAY YOUR GUILT... AND LIVE!

This book will help you know what to do when people create "obligations" and try to force them on you.

It will show you how to resist pressure, how to avoid being exploited by others out of a mistaken sense of politeness or responsibility.

It will tell you how to say "no" to unwarranted demands on your time, your energy, your emotions—and "yes" to the real you that longs for expression and fulfillment.

It can do for you what it has already done for hundreds of thousands of readers—give you a new outlook on life and a sense of freedom such as you have never felt before.

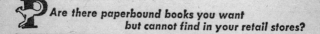
**Are there paperbound books you want
but cannot find in your retail stores?**

You can get any title in print in **POCKET BOOK** editions. Simply send retail price, local sales tax, if any, plus 35¢ per book to cover mailing and handling costs, to:

MAIL SERVICE DEPARTMENT
POCKET BOOKS • A Division of Simon & Schuster, Inc.
1230 Avenue of the Americas • New York, New York 10020

Please send check or money order. We cannot be responsible for cash.   *Catalogue sent free on request.*

Titles in this series are also available at discounts in quantity lots for industrial or sales-promotional use. For details write our Special Products Department: Department AR, POCKET BOOKS, 1230 Avenue of the Americas, New York, New York 10020.

The Art of Selfishness

by
David Seabury

A KANGAROO BOOK
PUBLISHED BY POCKET BOOKS NEW YORK

THE ART OF SELFISHNESS

Julian Messner edition published 1964

POCKET BOOK edition published September, 1974

4th printing.....................September, 1977

This POCKET BOOK edition includes every word contained in the original, higher-priced edition. It is printed from brand-new plates made from completely reset, clear, easy-to-read type.
POCKET BOOK editions are published by
POCKET BOOKS,
a Simon & Schuster Division of
GULF & WESTERN CORPORATION
1230 Avenue of the Americas,
New York, N.Y. 10020.
Trademarks registered in the United States
and other countries.

ISBN: 0-671-81729-9.

This POCKET BOOK edition is published by arrangement with Julian Messner. Copyright, 1937, by David Seabury, copyright, ©, 1964 by Evelyn Lewis. All rights reserved. This book, or portions thereof, may not be reproduced by any means without the permission of the original publisher: Julian Messner, a Simon & Schuster division of Gulf & Western Corporation, 1230 Avenue of the Americas, New York, N.Y. 10020.

Printed in the U.S.A.

Foreword

Ideas are magical. They lurk in the strangest places, and often the simplest of them can transform all life around them.

Benjamin Franklin sent up a kite; a French painter thought it might be nice if he could only capture on paper the picture his eye could see; Einstein had the curious notion that light somehow was bent as it travelled through space—and the lives of untold millions were each affected personally by these ideas as though someone had reached out and touched them directly.

Sometimes an idea can catch you at a crucial moment in your own life and jolt you out of a tailspin. Such an idea is the unorthodox thesis of this unusual book. It was first published in 1937. It ran through many editions, was listed as the top bestseller by *The New York Times* in November 1937, and remained in print in its original edition for eleven years. Subsequently it had a long life in some reprint editions.

One of the first reviews appeared in the Massachusetts *Springfield Union*, November 10, 1937, and what the reviewer, A. Corydon White, had to say was at that time quite surprising and is now worth repeating:

It may sound like sacrilege to say it, but this book could do more good in some homes than the Bible. It should be particularly valuable in those homes where there is in-law, relative, or general matrimonial discord. . . . From the thousands of cases which have passed through his hands as a practicing psychologist, Dr. Seabury has arrived at a theory of living which is at once sensible and logical.

Why has this book stood the test of time so well and helped so many? Because most of us run scared and haven't the courage to say "no" to people or situations that nag us or destroy us. We have been taught to feel guilty when we refuse someone's request no matter how preposterous, so we carry the world on our backs and suffer the tortures of the misguided "righteous." *The Art of Selfishness* gave us a defensive weapon.

The essential rightness of this book was confirmed in 1955 when Anne Lindbergh's beloved *Gift from the Sea* became a spectacular international bestseller. That exquisitely written book showed women how to get along with others and how to deal with the problems and pressures in their own lives. It helped them to achieve an inner harmony in the face of an outer discord, and it taught them how to do all this without feeling any shame about making the hard decisions that were called for if one wanted to live a good life.

But eighteen years before that, Dr. Seabury had already put his finger on the basic problem of interpersonal relations and had pointed out the startling but necessary solutions. It *was* a matter of selfishness. But whose? The answer he gave stirred up quite a bit of excitement because it did not "conform"—but it helped a lot of people see a way out of their own terrible dilemmas.

The original idea for this book was mine. I persuaded Dr. Seabury to write it because I felt it was a statement that needed desperately to be made, and that it would strike spark. Besides, I knew that Dr. Seabury had, from his vast private practice, the innumerable case histories that could elucidate the thesis and that he had the wisdom as well as the skill to make it appealing.

Why then a *revised* edition now? Because the specific references to events of the thirties are no longer pertinent; in some cases, they are incomprehensible. The changes I have made are few, and all of them have been checked and approved by Mrs. Evelyn Seabury—who was Dr. Seabury's skillful collaborator during the creation of all his books.

This book has done much good—but most of it quietly. Every now and then a reader would write to Dr. Seabury to thank him for the help the book had given, but otherwise there has been silence.

But in November of 1962 this silence was shattered. A famous Hollywood actress and television star who is now a great success (but prefers not to reveal her identity here) disclosed that she had stumbled over this book at what was, in her own words, a very low point in her life. She had found a battered, old copy of the book while rummaging through a second-hand bookshop. Something about the title intrigued her, probably because she had been brought up to believe otherwise, and the idea seemed shocking.

What she found as she flipped through its pages changed the whole course of her life. This was the notion that saved her from emotional confusion and despair:

Don't worry about the whole world: if you do it will overwhelm you. Worry about one wave at a time. Please yourself. Do something for you, and the rest will fall in line.

The idea appealed to her. Everything she did from that moment on had to be measured by the one rule: IS THIS GOOD FOR ME? If it was, no matter what others thought or said, she did it; if it was not, she just didn't!

"You can't imagine how calm and effective my life became as a result of applying this test," she explained. "*The Art of Selfishness* helped me over one of the worst periods of my own life. I am sure it can do the same for anyone else who reads it carefully, and carries out, with firmness and conviction, the startling but practical ideas it has to offer. It will take courage to do it, because people will talk—especially those who have been 'riding on your back.' But stay firm. Do what is good for *you*. Do this and you will discover, as I did, that what is good for you is invariably good for others."

The word "no," or the phrase "I won't do it," is a wonderful weapon in the arsenal of life. Here, then, is a manual for dealing with the problems of selfishness . . . *the selfishness. of others*. What *they* term selfishness is really their own, not yours. Once you learn that, you are on the way to an uncluttered and joyful life.

AARON SUSSMAN

Contents

Foreword   v

Introduction: Challenge of the Hour   1

CHAPTER

1. The Pressures of Living   7
   (Never free from burdens) Hal and
   Meg Dever in a personal Quandary

2. The Key to Your Problems   12
   The world you are up against

3. Never Compromise Yourself   16
   How John Constable found a new
   job, and why

4. Taught to Fail   19
   Peter Coe has a troublesome history

5. Love and Duty   22
   Jane, a musician (singer), becomes
   pregnant

6. Which Way Happiness?   25
   Dr. Saisis has family troubles

7. The Better Laziness   29
   Elwood Winters learns new types of
   management

8. A Way That Wins   34
   How Parmella Steadman became attractive

9. No Ego Satisfactions   38
   How Horace Headlison, educator, loses his job and why

10. A New Golden Rule   43
    Mr. Judson gets a jolt

11. Know Your Own Mind   49
    Why you need to discover yourself

12. Death Takes No Holiday   55
    Eric Jurgeson is faced with heart failure

13. How to Refuse a Request   58
    Ross Lowman learns to say no

14. Is Self-Protection Right?   65
    Mr. Barnaby takes his wife in hand

15. The Wisdom of Life   68
    How to handle contrary people

16. When Sacrifice Does Harm   72
    Mrs. Farwell ruins her son

17. Greed Is Stupid   75
    Banker Enrod comes to a bad end

18. Control Your Enemies   79
    Mr. Dugan is conquered and dies. Was it murder?

19. Medicine for a Martinet   82
    How a family handled a dominator

20. Correcting a Nuisance   87
    How to eliminate your irritations

21. The Higher Selfishness   93
    A businesswoman learns a lesson

22. Ways Out of Loneliness   97
    Caroline Fenway makes friends

23. On Being Engaged   100
    *The same young woman doesn't
    know whom she loves*

24. Arts of Human Appeal   106
    A salesman in a dilemma

25. Business Faces a Crisis   111
    *A manufacturing company in a bad
    fix*

26. Love Isn't Enough   117
    *Why Bert Fredrickson has always
    failed*

27. How Trouble Grows   120
    *How stealthily a situation overcame
    Mr. Watson*

28. How to Handle Gossip   125
    Four men in the same predicament

29. A Marriage Dilemma   129
    The wife's side. Kate comes to a crisis

30. Whiskey in Its Place   134
    Eugene Bartow has a drink problem

31. Sexual Maladjustment   137
    *A marriage problem from the man's
    side*

32. How to Avoid Suicide   145
Why Frank Dural took his own life

33. Nerves on Edge   149
The troubles of Mr. Gault and others

34. Inside a Difficulty   154
Should Henry Harding resign?

35. Why Hardships Are So Hard   160
A percent report on 1000 cases, as to kinds of trouble found

36. Where Sorrow Ends   166
How to put yourself in order

37. Secrets in Divorce   170
What to do and why

38. Two Sides of One Picture   176
Finding the realities in a love tangle

39. New Skills for Quarreling   182
Louise Godwin has an argument

40. Why Die Young?   188
Evans Strickland is exhausted

41. They Laugh Who Sleep   192
Mrs. Durston learns to relax

42. In Sickness and Health   196
How to deal with physical difficulties

43. When Worried About Money   200
You—when troubled by expense

44. How to Be Rich and Like It   204
The problem of investment hits Peter Pauling

45. The Habit of Success   207
How Norbert Wales found his work

46. Accept Your Mistakes   213
Clara Atwater gives up remorse

47. How to Face a Crisis   219
Eight ways to overcome trouble

48. Easier Ways of Living   228
Twenty-two ways to simplify your life

49. A New Bill of Rights   238
Our rights to privacy and expansion

50. Your Place in Life   249
How to achieve dynamic living

The Art of
Selfishness

Introduction

Challenge of the Hour

If there is any way to live without having to make such a fuss about it, most of us want to know what it is. Mystics may talk of rewards in the hereafter, savants discuss Latin derivatives and the fourth dimension. We who struggle in everyday life wish some remedy for trouble in the here and now.

How close can we come to joy, how far away from pain? That is the question. It may be nobler to suffer the slings and arrows of outrageous fortune, but it's not to our liking, and anyway those instruments of death are out of date.

There ought to be something on the human side as efficient as machine guns to defend us against the horde of bothers that crowd us in office, home and street. We've been oppressed too long. We'd like some way to overcome the odds of a greedy world.

Are there any? None, according to pessimists. You must bear your burdens, cry the moralists. It's that kind of world, sophisticates maintain.

I'm not convinced, however, that the intelligence which split the atom and is sending man into outer space is incapable of discovering ways to live more easily.

If our social forms had changed as rapidly as our material structure, all might have been well. As it is, our mechanics belong to the present, our financial and

1

social ethics to the past. We are culturally and politically a thousand years behind man's needs. We cannot go on in so top-heavy an environment. We must give up our mechanics or improve our conventions.

I wonder how you meet your troubles. Do you get along with your relatives more comfortably than your ancestors did? Are the children simpler to handle? Is your job less tiring than skinning a bear? Are the taxes easier to pay than tribute money?

People suggest we have become a soft nation because of civilized luxuries. I doubt it. I don't believe we're civilized. We've made an objective structure of office buildings and subways for barbarians to push about in. We've fashioned a set of laws and a pseudo morality that requires us to ape Loyola, trying to deny ourselves as he did, when we don't feel like serfs of virtue.

If we are savages at heart, we'll get nowhere walking around in angelic costumes, flapping our wings to cover our depredations. We'll go further with honesty and an ethics suitable to our caste.

A serious factor in life nowadays is that many of our superstitions stand as directly in the way of our conquering troubles as they did centuries ago. What would you think of a man if he had himself stood on his head and let his eye be gouged out to cure the gout? That was a method in vogue at the time the customs were established that you have followed in handling your problems.

Once upon a time, to propitiate the gods, men performed strange rites, and lived in terror of taboos. Today the god of opinion, *What-will-people-think?*, works just as much mischief. In countries where flies were sacred, it was a sin to kill them. In consequence, germs spread everywhere. Children lay writhing in fever from the ravages of disease. In America, many a problem is unsolvable because of similar taboos. You cannot deal with the germs of incompatibility or the pressure of predatory intimates. Sentimentality stands in the way.

Once upon a time, in a supposed worship of God, society might have required you to sacrifice your children on the altar. Now, you must sacrifice them in the name of quasi unselfishness, allowing some virulent influence to stay in your home, when you know their tender minds are injured. Fear of claiming your rights is today as insane a frenzy as ever ruled "the heather." No juggernaut took greater toll.

The next step in human progress is to dump the load of sanctified idiocy we miscall our moral values, and accept the principles of nature. Man has done this in mechanical and scientific realms. We don't believe in a river Styx and a special hell under Wall Street to which its gangsters go. Nor do we expect to fall off the edge of the earth.

We've given up superstition in the physical area. But if you mention to a fear-ridden follower of the conventions the thought of discarding the sanctions of the Dark Ages, ideals of conduct that came into being when it was considered a sin to unravel the mysteries of life, you shock his sensibilities. He looks at you sad-eyed and shakes his head.

This arrogant egotism is the worst trait in human beings. It kills all prophets who challenge its stupidities. It is willing to accept the foolishness that injured other generations. Its own conventions alone are right.

This was once the attitude toward matters of science as well. It still dominates in economics and the law.

Only as ignorance has given place to fact has trouble been overcome. No people has long endured which has not rid itself of antiquated ways. Plowing with a piece of wood, or crossing a river on a log, was useful in its day. Slavery had its merits. Incest, practiced for centuries, may at times have saved humanity. To worship a wooden god was better than irreligion.

Shall we then maintain a custom because it has served? That is the attitude in the moral realm.

Many otherwise intelligent people still deny the rights of self and quite as blatantly mistake the nature of trouble. They believe man's character is evil and as such should be suppressed. They treat misfortune as a punishment for wrong-doing, a discipline meted out by God upon a throne to his rebellious subjects.

That germs exist is a misfortune. To have deserts to cross in order to reach verdant fields, forests to clear to raise grain, is trouble. No one made it so in order to punish us. Life is constituted on cosmic principles. Our difficulties lie in overcoming the raw realities of nature. Nor is this less true of equally primitive forces in human nature. The digging of soil and the cultivation of consciousness are the ends of effort, science and art. Every winged victory comes out of the ground.

In this threatening period no conquest is possible if we do not use the same spirit in understanding the problems of man's thought that we have so nobly revealed in the control of material substance. We must use the selfsame purpose that has harnessed the forces of nature if we would regenerate and direct the powers of man. Not otherwise will humanity avoid self-destruction.

This means that we must master and obey two great principles, applying them in everyday experience. The first I would call the Basic Law of Being, the second the Magic Formula of Human Relations. You'll admit that to be content within yourself and to be at peace with your fellows are major aims in life.

One can put the Basic Law into three words: NEVER COMPROMISE YOURSELF. No matter what the situation, how pressing the problem, never give up your integrity. When you do, you make more sorrow than when you don't, hurting everyone in the end.

The Magic Formula is also a three-word principle: NO EGO SATISFACTIONS. Never exalt yourself and vent your emotions to inflate your mind or magnify your pride against life. To win, you must obey nature. Her will, not yours, is omnipotent.

This is not a surrender to prejudice, nor a return to the values of antiquity. It is of science and with science. To be happy, we must discover what life is and how it operates. A continual uncovering of truth for subjective expansion is quite as essential as in mechanical action. Power is a matter of cosmic law; morality, when right, is in harmony with natural phenomena.

To bring this conclusion from the level of speculation to the testing laboratory of daily experience, let us suppose that you are considering some vital step in your life: going to college, selecting a vocation, choosing a wife or trying to settle a strike. How would you have gone at your task in the old days?

Was not learning in the Middle Ages an artificial matter, without much relation to reality? And as to your work, you selected a vocation after the pattern of your family: knight, page, artisan's apprentice or serf. Considerations of your abilities and constitution did not enter. A wife? She was "the baggage." You married for a hundred external reasons—from family to fornication. If ennobled, it was arranged; when at the peasant level, it was enforced. Love had little to do with it. No one conciliated the mob or considered its will. One put opponents to the sword.

This solution is still followed in certain lands. Nor is marriage as a matter of barter, or vocation by parental edict, extinct. Even our colleges smell of the mustiness of superstition. But change is upon us. The greatest transition man has ever seen is taking place. Knowledge is pushing tradition out. Character is measuring the fitness for work. Love is slowly becoming the reason for sex and parenthood. A glimmer of social justice, a passing of the despots, is taking place.

Should we not in our own lives make this mighty step, this crossing of the threshold from the darkness of ignorance to the enlightenment of a natural world? Should we not put obedience to cosmic law and bionomic principles (by which one means ways of life that are natural and discovered by scientific seeking) in place of the oblique prejudices that ruin our days? This decision each man must make for himself.

Behind war and international questions is that of the integrity of peoples: the right to be themselves, unmolested and unenslaved. Within this and beyond it is a mightier question: the right of any class to live and work, unmolested and unenslaved. We are on the battlefield of this great issue.

Nor is this struggle for the law of integrity—Never Compromise Yourself, as a person, as a class, as a people—the only world issue. Mutual aid and cooperation, those formative principles of human relations, those fulfillments of the Magic Formula, all these are equally at the front in our crisis. They contest the greed that has ruled trade and tradition until now. The right to live, the right to love: these are the battle cries.

Shall we, in our personal lives, follow the old or the new ways? Shall we continue as slaves of decadent conventions, or take a place as self-respecting men upon earth.

And as to the worship of avarice that brings such toil and trouble, shall we supplant it with mutual aid, establishing the art of cooperation in our homes, among our kindred and in our social practices, or keep the envies and fears that heretofore have shaped our destinies? Those are the questions—as challenging for you and me as for a troubled world.

1   *The Pressures of Living*

You know how a man feels when troubles crowd and press, when after a day of routine he looks at life with harsh awareness. The monotony of effort is overpowering.

It was late July and sticky hot. The edge of the wall cut the river in two. Dull red bricks, seamed and sooty, formed part of Hal Dever's view. On the left, sunlight sparkled on the water and shone on distant hills. To the right, gloom and grime.

His life was like that, Hal thought, except that the flatness of civilization was more than half of it. A little of his vision had some of nature left, a few trees and a bit of sky, but the rest: monotony and cement.

It wasn't the desolation of duty that appalled. He could bear his work, dull as it was. Never to be free of pressure, to carry his family on his back, was another matter. He'd been doing it for years, so patiently that each month added to his burden.

If Nellie, his daughter, quarreled with her mother, she would wait for him at the front door ready to engage his allegiance against her maternal foe. If Jack had difficulty in school, his father must tutor him. Hal's brother drove down to the office to be first for his services. His mother, however, asserted a prior claim. Hal was bone of her bone and, come what may, should live for her.

He straightened his tie and closed his desk. Well, time to go; no use looking at that view. His family would have to wait tonight; hours more of business to finish. He grabbed up his papers: a sausage advertisement, one for patent medicine, the layout for a toilet soap and his cigarette account. The stuff he'd attended to for years.

Ashamed of tears in his eyes, Hal hurried to the elevator. Ever since he was a boy, something had been wrong with his life. No matter how he tried, he couldn't get out of strain. He did what he could for people, but they weren't satisfied. He was their drudge, never an equal, seldom a friend.

Hal, as a boy, had dreamed of being an artist, of painting the limitless sky and the meditating trees. He'd toiled to tint his brush with the haunting pigments of beauty. In his brain moved a dynamic symmetry. He saw his canvases as messages to lure men from the drabness of their ways.

Years passed, a girl had smiled, a ceremony was said. The painter disappeared in the businessman peddling his amputated art to pay for rent, dishes, onions, new hats, the needs of each approaching baby. He toiled under pressure, worrying about the situation, in conflict over a thousand encroachments on his life.

His thought, once direct and clear, was circular and crooked. Sometimes he lay in bed, his brain in a whirl, thinking of the problems he couldn't meet. His relation to himself, his career, his marriage; everything was caught in the mesh of involvement. Yet these were not the worries that seared his soul. A morbid, moribund anguish locked his brain in torpor. He raged that life should be spent in this senseless way. At eighty he'd find himself carrying the same load.

Creative natures are not alone in such brooding. Life does not select idealists as her only victims, though society likes to destroy them. Nor is the struggle masculine. Fate enslaves her own sex, even when a man is the economic reed to which it clings. Women know their gamut of weariness. The problem of keeping a male as security is not all of it; there come periods in which the bonds of intimacy yield small dividends, while the expense of spiritual upkeep is great. It was like this with Hal's wife.

Meg had to be Hydra-headed and many-handed enough to spend each penny with the skill of a Shylock, do a million details about the house, yet nurse her husband and babies as well. Her troubles were those of five ordinary persons in a less dizzy world.

It seldom occurred to Hal that Meg bore a burden greater than his own. Did he not earn her livelihood? Was she not in the home, protected and free to "use her time as she chose"?

Only those who are placed in a position to know from contact with both sides of such a situation ever gain a true perspective. Suppose Hal had been so intimate with you that he felt impelled to tell his story. Would he have painted a gray picture of his wife's pressure, or spoken only of his own? Let us imagine that she was your friend, and in one of those times when her mood was close, she described her endless dilemmas. Would you have guessed how Hal struggled? Each would have given the feeling of being misunderstood. Too much was required of them. Neither had freedom. A little bridge, a dance, the theater, that was all. Communication was rare between them. Responsibility kept them under.

With the feeling of slavery to work, Hal would have told you of his wife's extravagance and the snobbishness of her family, how she permitted insubordination in the children, yet dominated him herself. She never let him alone, yet he couldn't stand her neglect after one of their quarrels. He was sure she no longer loved him. There wasn't much use keeping on.

Meg would have spoken of being overworked, bothered by inconveniences and by living in a neighborhood she couldn't stand. She had a feeling of futility. Her faith in people, life and religion was gone.

Is this an exaggerated picture? You know it is not. You can duplicate it in your neighborhood, among your friends and maybe in your home. It is American life, at least a goodly part of it; not as it appears to sentimentalists, not as casual observers know it, but as those who touch the core of things have found it to be.

And the cause? *Fear!* Fear of selfishness. Fear of being and doing as nature does. Fear of living according to one's kind. Compromise of self, of love, of life.

Cynicism is a pressing question. What shall we do with our doubt? How shall we avoid futility: that dry rot creeping up the spine of youth?

If Hal felt much of his effort was "useless," Meg realized the sacrifices they had made were wasted. Hal's brother was no more adjusted, despite all that had been done for him; Nellie no stronger or finer because of their sacrifice. Nor had she, Meg, by enduring the jealousy of Hal's mother, done anything but suffer. The foundations on which these two depended were falling into dust.

Failure of life on the pattern we have worshiped, despair in the face of a false ethic, these are spreading unhappiness in every home. The burden of duty on the basis of unselfishness is destroying the world. It makes people:

Accept the presence of a relative they can't in the end endure.

Live in a neighborhood that offends their beings.

Take a job that goes against the grain.

Marry a person they no longer love from fear of causing hurt.

Maintain a relationship they cannot bear because to get out of it seems ruthless.

Accept a responsibility that constricts usefulness and compromises the future.

Work beyond their strength to support someone in luxury.

Take people on as a burden, who could take care of themselves.

Deny the expansion of personal gifts because their development seems "impractical."

Let intimates nag or dominate in order to keep the peace.

Do things against the feeling of integrity because someone thinks they should.

Deny basic needs to obey archaic conventions.

In the end, if we yield to such timidity, we make more sorrow than if we follow our own desires. Fear of self is the greatest of all terrors, the deepest of all dreads, the commonest of all mistakes. From it grows failure. Because of it, life is a mockery. Out of it comes despair.

There is no fact, no interest, no concern more important to your happiness than this. To break from the jail of circumstance, you must take your courage in hand. But let us understand each other. This new liberty is not anarchy. There is no counseling of greed, of lust, of licentiousness in the attitudes of science. We are not justifying the frenzies of our age.

Nor do we defend the barbaric ruthlessness so apparent in young people these days: that careless selfishness that tramples the flowers in your garden, runs your car into a ditch, mocks you for your sentiments and derides your faith in God.

The rampant egotism of our day is not the product of a better ethic. It comes from the absence of any controls.

Youth has rebelled against the shrunken values of its elders. It is too often footloose, sex-mad and crassly indifferent. Riotous arrogance and rapacious rebellion are not constructive selfishness—they are insanity.

2   *The Key to Your Problems*

Each of us, through some part of his life, is pursued by trouble.

No matter what wealth or position is ours, fatigue inevitably appears. Details of home and business, the greed of relatives and the mischief of children, all these cause strain. None of us escapes.

Are such bothers avoidable? Can life be made an easier experience? Or are there troubles attendant upon the very act of living; part, shall we say, of the play and interplay of normal independence? I wish to do this, you to do that. Our purposes at times collide. We do not want to hurt each other, but wish still more to act as we choose. As difficulty is part of nature, so inconvenience may spring from the very fact of individual desire.

For years I have asked a question that bears on this point. A young boy, traveling with his parents, was separated from them and did not communicate for days. They searched for him anxiously. When discovered, he paid little attention to the sorrow his absence had caused. Was this conduct selfish or unselfish?

"If he'd been my boy, I'd have shown him," many have answered.

When I suggest that my friends read how Jesus in his youth lingered with the wise men in the temple, they are less vocal. Sometimes I've told another story of an unmarried man who, forsaking his trade, left home without saying where he was going. When his mother and her family went looking for him, he spoke questioningly of their right to do so. Was his conduct selfish? "Who is my mother, and who are my brethren?" is a potent query.

This man became involved with the authorities. They considered his activities revolutionary. An arrest led to his death. He did not at any time limit his conduct out of consideration for his relatives.

People are told to follow in the footsteps of Jesus; to shape their behavior upon his. Ethical leaders hold before their followers his consecration to duty as he saw it. I have yet to find those who consider the whole picture. His relation to his family is ignored.

The reason for this neglect is not hard to understand. No one could follow him and fulfill our moral code. The two are incompatible.

Someday, in an urge to conquer trouble, we shall learn the part unselfishness plays in hindering us: unselfishness as advocated in our time. We shall see its relation to the flood of mental breakdowns, trace its influence in divorce. We shall know how it drives men to crime, and find it a cause of suicide. At their worst, greed and envy have not wrought such havoc as rejection.

The successful handling of everyday problems is difficult until we understand this enigma and how wisely to direct ourselves in the situations we meet. The key to most difficulties does not lie in the dilemmas themselves, but in our relation to them.

It is, moreover, our wits we must think with; our bodies we must use to produce good results. Neglect of ourselves as persons leads to ineffectuality. More than this,

. 14   THE ART OF SELFISHNESS

many acts of apparent unselfishness, when viewed in terms of the ultimate outcome, prove to bring sorrow to those for whom the sacrifice was made.

Good and evil are not matters of a moment. Wisdom and foolishness are measured by the developments of years. Conduct is wise or foolish only in reference to its results.

Neither selfishness nor unselfishness, when truly applied, has to do with your relation to another person. They pertain to life. When understood, both are good and beautiful.

If you do not concern yourself with being a vital force, you cannot serve the world in which you live. You become a burden. Constructive self-preservation is man's first duty. Without it, life makes parasites of us.

Everything that lives, from the moment it comes into being, seeks its nourishment and continues so to seek. The food of a man is emotional and mental as well as physical. He who does not ask, even demand, his right to special nourishment sickens and becomes a burden by the measure in which he denies his birthright. There is no wise unselfishness without basic self-concern, no permanent power for goodness if the organism which fulfills that goodness is limited or injured. *Your duty is to yourself.*

It is provable that a true ethical structure and every vitality of religion builds on this forthright doctrine. Dr. Pierre Janet has said that no man is normal who does not love his psyche. He cannot otherwise keep himself in order as a useful citizen. Nor is this true of humanity alone. It is a cosmic principle. The worth of a cabbage depends upon the way it fulfills a promise in the seed. The value of a cow inheres in her health and development. The service of each creature lies in this selfishness.

When denial constricts this duty of an organism to be itself, it is against life and as such becomes evil.

The surrender of the least of one's primary rights leads to some measure of corruption before the span of life is over. The duty to others is achieved only by being what one can become as radiantly as possible.

This is why Dr. Janet counseled the self-love that protects and develops one's attributes. Such a higher selfishness is identical with religious reverence, but hatred of one's self is tantamount to blaming the Creator for one's nature. Condemnation of self and condemnation of God are one and the same. Gratitude for the qualities of self and acceptance of the responsibility of life are simple forms of worship.

Consideration of this principle is essential to the understanding of difficulties. It is the key to our problems. We cannot otherwise avoid the influence of the antiquated ideas about us. People do not know that when unselfishness is true it is not a sacrifice but a proper use of self in obedience to cosmic laws.

He is unselfish who yields to universal principles and willingly obeys their laws, scientifically discovered and repetitively proved. He is greedy who takes from society more than he gives to it, living on an income he miscalls his own. He is truly unselfish if day by day he does those things nature endowed him to do, fulfilling his constructive possibilities. He is falsely selfish if he refuses the hard way when it requires him to conquer his self-indulgent attributes. He is altruistic even if in self-mastery he goes against the wishes of family, friends and all who suffer because of his integrity.

Years ago, I decided to go abroad in preparation for my vocation. My mother was sixty-two. Eight of her friends wrote reminding me she was well along in years, and pleading with me not to leave until she died. She passed away at the age of ninety-three. The writers of those letters condemned me as selfish because I left as I did. My mother suffered to have her wishes disregarded, but told me a few weeks before she died that one of the best things I had ever done for her was to leave her when and as I did.

Had I not gone, it is obvious I would have begun my training in the fifties. I would have carried in my heart a grievance more hurtful to our relation than my absence. I could not have been the financial and spiritual support my profession made possible.

3   *Never Compromise Yourself*

John Constable had come to the end of everything. Two violent interviews had taken place that day: one with his employer, one with his wife. Both had ended disastrously. John at the moment was pacing a station platform about to board a train. He wasn't running away, nor leaving as an act of choice. There wasn't anything else to do. He had a chance to secure a new job in the Middle West. The father of a college chum was president of a corporation that might employ him. He wasn't sorry to go, after Ethel's words. In her eyes he was a failure.

"You are never willing to do what's expected of you," she had said.

He couldn't, in this instance at least. To produce the formula Scodnar and Snell had asked for was out of the question. He'd worked as their chemical engineer for twelve years. He'd done questionable things too:

made stuff that couldn't last, and helped them amass a fortune. This last product they wanted him to concoct was sheer murder.

"You've always refused to play the game," Ethel's eyes had blazed as she said it, "and in consequence we've never gotten on. Five men from minor positions in the company have been promoted over you in the last seven years. Business is business, and you know it. You've been just as stupid and selfish here at home. How do you expect us to get into the Bayfield Country Club if you won't go out with me to the dances and dinners and card parties as the other men do. It's a shame. You've ruined everything with your horrid indifference."

So that's what it had come to. He'd tried to fit in. He'd gone, too—plenty of times. Bitterly, John recalled occasions when he'd done his best to be a success according to the Bayfield pattern.

Two long years of work came and went before John Constable was in a position to send for his wife and children. Money had gone to them regularly; he'd been accepted and had prospered in the new company. He had, in fact, begun his contact with them by selling them an invention of his own that Scodnar and Snell had thought too expensive to manufacture. The royalties from the new firm's use of his creation promised to make him wealthy.

It wasn't his financial independence, however, that caused the change in the tone of John's letters to his wife. He was a transformed man. He told her, moreover, that their reunion, as far as he was concerned, must take place on a basis they had never before enjoyed.

"I've discovered *the cause of failure*, both in work and intimacy," he wrote. "It comes from one of two mistakes. *One either doesn't compromise enough, or else too much.* Every man who wants to succeed must choose for himself which way he wishes to go. All my life, up to two years ago, I lost out by being unwilling to go whole hog in the ways of getting what I wanted. I couldn't be ruthless in winning wealth. I compromised most of the time, in halfhearted ways. I never dared to be myself, or to stand up for my integrities. Now, I've taken this latter course. I'm through, utterly through, with compromise. This company is one of the few I've found where stark integrity is appreciated. They don't put any pressure on me except to use my wits. I'm first of all a scientific man in their eyes, here to develop the usefulness of their products.

"I've found a group of friends, too, who accept me for what I am. If you want to bring the children and join me on this basis, I want you to come. But not otherwise."

That Ethel decided to go to her husband spoke for the remnant of flame we may have buried somewhere under the clutter of our social masquerade. That she fitted in and enjoyed the adventure gave more assurance of her latent womanhood.

Sooner or later, we each must make the choice that came to John and Ethel. Nothing in the setting of civilization requires us to follow their example. Success of a sort and the solution of many of our problems is possible by the acceptance of compromise and the discarding of the honesties. For a while at least, one "gets by" with arrogance and chicanery, beating others by competitive shrewdness and outmaneuvering them in cunning. John might have made just as much money and won social recognition had he stayed with Scodnar and Snell, inventing products to cheat the public. He could have done it—*if he had been that sort of man.*

The art of overcoming obstacles is not a matter of

morals but of character and consistency. We conquer trouble when we discover what we are like and decide to follow a way of life that matches our natures. *Frustration appears if we live and act on half measures.*

4   *Taught to Fail*

Some years ago I sat talking with a man we shall call Peter Coe. The line of the Rockies stretched before us. The sky was brilliant with clouds.

"It's strange," Coe mused, "that I was actually taught to become a failure. I suppose my story isn't extraordinary, except that it came out all right."

"How were you taught to fail?" I asked.

"By being made to doubt myself, and even to fear myself," came the answer. "It began in my childhood. My parents adored an older brother. He was one of those curlyheads, who wiggle everything until it goes their way. I was made to sacrifice for him on all occasions. It was Percy this and Percy that. I believed it my duty to keep it up. I worked at home while he went to college. When girls came into my life, I was shy and uncertain. I fell in love, but mother didn't like Helen. She convinced me it was my duty to stay with her. Father wasn't well and soon died.

"After some years mother changed her mind and decided I ought to marry. She picked out the daughter of her oldest friend. I objected at first. Agnes was nice enough, but I didn't love her. Mother talked and wept.

'It would be such a good match,' she said, 'and make her so happy.' Besides, Agnes' mother owned part of father's business that I then managed, and we'd keep more money in the family. I yielded in the end, as I always had. It seemed selfish not to."

"But your wife loved you, didn't she?" I queried.

"Loved me! She had no chance. She was as much under her mother as I was under mine. And, Heavens, how I hated her."

"Your wife?"

"No, my mother-in-law. She used to tell Agnes every day how much she'd suffered to bring her into the world. That was a lie, and she knew it. Most children come as the result of amative life, not from a horrible nobility. And anyway, the poor child had no say about it. There's something ghastly about good women like my mother-in-law. You know the kind I mean. They practice such self-denial they can't do anything efficiently.

"Mrs. Bassy talked and talked about self-sacrifice, but she was selfish to the bone. She had to be, she'd become so dependent. She'd destroyed the life of her oldest children; stultified them with her possessiveness until one died of pneumonia and the other barely earned his salt, one of those echoes of a man. She demanded, however, that Agnes sacrifice for her, and Agnes' way was to make *me* do it. The women kept house for me."

"The three Fates," I murmured.

"No, sir. That's what they thought they were and intended to be, but life fooled them. You see, there's something resilient and resistant in human nature, and destiny is often kind to us when we think she's being terrible. Anyway, there I was with a wife I admired but didn't love, a home I revered but didn't like, two mothers I respected and secretly hated. I had inherited my job and was totally unfit for it. All of it happened in the name of duty. Heavens, what an evil word. *Duty!*

Most duties are desecrations of all that is beautiful."

I nodded: "They aren't duties, only ignorant superstitions."

"They destroy just the same, as long as we believe in them. But fate was kind to me. The business failed under my mismanagement. That left us almost penniless. I became ill with tuberculosis and nearly died. A distant relative offered me a cottage on his Colorado ranch, and there I went—alone. It took me five years to get well. My wife and our mothers had to go to work. That was their salvation; being out in the world, meeting people, two of them fell in love."

"Which two?" I asked.

"My wife and my mother." He chuckled. "Yes, sir, my wife and my mother. It happened to Agnes first, after I'd been away three years and wasn't progressing very rapidly. She wrote she wanted a divorce. Then I began to get well. The next year mother wrote she too had found her man. It's surprising how rapidly I improved from then on. There wasn't any reason for me to go back after that, so I decided to keep a continent between us.

"The point of my story is this. If nature hadn't stepped in and made the business fail because I wasn't fitted for it, and then made me sick, I'd have felt it my duty to stick it out in a situation that was wrong from start to finish. Not a single good thing came from that attitude. It made misery. Our spoiling of my brother ruined him. He got in with a sporty crowd, began to drink and ended on drugs. He'd never had to restrain himself. And look at the suffering that came to both our families because I married Agnes. No, sir, in the end it causes trouble if you do anything against yourself."

"What should you have done?" I asked.

"First, disobeyed my parents every time they tried

to make me into my brother's slave. Second, refused to go into father's business, which I hated. Third, gone away to get the type of education I needed. I'm a commercial designer now, and could have gone further if I'd gotten into art school. Fourth, I oughtn't to have married Agnes, no matter how mother fussed; and fifth, I should have married Helen, whom I'd loved all my boyhood. Won't you come out to the house to meet her? She's my wife now."

I went, to witness for once a happy marriage; joy at the end of a long, long journey.

5   *Love and Duty*

She was pregnant. There was no doubt of it. A feeling of dread came over Jane. Something seemed to stand there in the dark threatening her. She felt its fingers reaching to grasp her throat. She could not breathe. A wave of nausea, then a chill. She must pull herself together.

For an hour she sat motionless, thinking. Swivie, the cat, got up and stretched. Snowflakes pattered against the window. Someone shook the furnace. She was pregnant —pregnant—and what should she do?

It wasn't that she didn't want a child. All three years of her marriage she and Tom had talked about it. But the problems were so great, and there was the question of her career. That, after all, was the real issue. Twelve years of preparation, twelve years of the hardest kind

of work, and her mother would have her give it up—
whissh—just like that, as if it had been play.

She wouldn't have said that about Tom's vocation, and
he hadn't spent a third of the time in getting ready to
do something worthwhile in life. Tom—oh, Tom must
go on. Tom must be spared anything that would dis-
rupt his success. Tom was a man.

"You are a strange, selfish woman," her mother had
said, "a strange, selfish woman to want to keep on with
your singing now that you have a husband and are
to have a child."

Was she? Jane wondered. Some assurance in her whis-
pered: NO. Her mother's ideas seemed abhorrent. She
saw a vision of herself plodding along like a patient
uterus, with no more brains than that. It made her
shiver. And what did it lead to? Painfully she counted
over the women she knew who had been unselfish after
her mother's pattern.

There was Mrs. Furriton. She'd been a lot of fun
as a classmate at college, and a brilliant girl too. Now
you couldn't get an idea out of her. Didies, dishes
and doilies—that was all. Mabel Saulter was somewhat
better, but you felt as if it were a desperate veneer, a
brave but hopeless attempt to keep in the human race
and feel the throb of things. She could chatter about the
political situation and tell of the scientific discoveries
with the best, but something had happened. She wasn't
the Mabel of yore.

Jane didn't argue to herself that every woman ought
to have a career, not that. But it shouldn't be torn
away from her after years and years of getting ready
for it. And then to have the glorious experience of being married, and having a child, made into a sodden
duty. That was what hurt. It took all the joy out of
giving to have cruel virtue piled on it. There was some-

thing so wonderful, so natural about it left untarnished by the denial people preached.

And wasn't it possible to have one's children and yet go on with one's career? Schumann-Heink, Louise Homer, lots of them had done it. She—Jane—got no further. The door opened. Tom burst in, energy and anger on his face.

"Hello, girl. Say but I'm glad to see you. I've been delayed, talking with your father, and of all—" he paused, not wishing to hurt his wife by the epithets that seemed to fit her family. "The old man tells me I should make you give up your career. He seems to hate the idea of it—talks about your duty. Do you know, there's something awful about such an attitude."

A wave of wild joy seized Jane. She leaped across the room into his arms.

"Oh, Tom, Tom, to hear you say that. It isn't the music only, although I want to keep it, I've worked so hard. It's the way they have of being so cruel and posing as so good. I'm not being selfish, I'm not."

"Of course you're not, darling," he cried, patting her gently. "We're not living in their century, and there isn't any such conflict between love and duty as they picture. It's only a superstitious bugaboo. Any woman has a right to go on with work and to keep her career, if it's only selling pins at the five-and-ten."

"She isn't any good, either, if she compromises," Jane looked up at him, "and she needn't go out of the home, or do anything especially. It's an attitude I'm fighting for. It's the right to be myself and not an institution. I don't want to be just your wife, or a mother, or a housekeeper, or anything else but myself. It's not a career that matters; I could give that up. I can't give up being Jane—and that's what they want me to do. I see it now. I see what's happened to the women who become submerged in—in duty. They compromise themselves, destroy their sex appeal, becoming half-alive sort of creatures. I'll never do it, never."

Tom held her close. "I'm with you, darling. I've been thinking a bit too. I've an idea. Do you know the greatest cause of divorce in America?"

"No, what?"

"Unselfishness, unselfishness as advocated by people like your parents. Women disappear under it. The girl the fellow married is gone. He only has something left they call—a-a—"

"A mother," Jane burst in, "a housekeeper, an institution. That's it. The men leave an institution—and I don't blame them."

6   Which Way Happiness?

Dr. Saisis left his laboratory with a glow of satisfaction on his face. His research in biochemistry was progressing. It seemed as if he would soon contribute another curative agent for the control of disease.

He looked about him as he strode along in the brisk autumn air. Life was good, he mused, as he watched a ferry moving across the Hudson. What a future lay ahead for humanity. He saw man overcoming difficulty after difficulty by means of more and more knowledge of life. An almost holy reverence for the spirit of science possessed him.

An hour later, Saisis entered his home. Cries greeted his ears. He heard his brother, speaking in firm admonishment. Then came the querulous voice of his Aunt Eliza. One of the children must have—Dr. Saisis got no further. His wife appeared in the hall, her eyes ablaze. They glared at him accusingly.

Saisis pulled himself together. His dreams departed for some sanctum where he kept them stored. He hadn't done anything, but he knew from long experience that he was somehow responsible for the scene upstairs.

"What's wrong," he asked, feeling his way.

"Carl has decided to marry that Carraway girl." Mrs. Saisis' voice was harsh.

"Well, why shouldn't he?" the father asked mildly. "He loves her."

"And he's going to take that position in South America."

"Well, why shouldn't he?" the doctor repeated. "He's fitted for it."

"He's letting the Carraways pay for his steamer fare."

"Well, why shouldn't they? They can well afford it."

"John Henry, you make me furious. She's older than he is, she's a divorcée. Carl is obligated to his uncle now that he's in his business, and as for accepting charity—I can't understand you. You've made your boy a selfish, conceited upstart, with your scientific ideas."

"So it seems," muttered John Saisis mildly and hurried to his study.

What was there he could have said to his wife to change the situation? She was not trying to live life on an orderly basis, or to solve her family's difficulties. *Millions don't want to correct their troubles. They wish to have their own way.* They do not see that the laws of life must be obeyed and increasingly discovered, in exactly the spirit in which modern science strives to know them.

In other words, the principles of order that engineers follow must be seen and fulfilled in your personal life as they are accepted by an Edison, or followed by a great composer, a skillful designer, a true artist. Life, thus lived, is a creative experience. It permits no successful deviation from basic law. You cannot be ugly in your handling of events without being repaid in kind at the end.

There are, I suppose, four sorts of men on earth: ruthless egotists, who take the way of greed; virtuous conventionalists, who follow the creeds; the blind rebels, who will not yield to any rules; and the men of science, who strive to obey natural law.

There is no meeting point between the old and the new attitudes in the face of life's problems. We go two roads. Those who revere the "good old ways" follow the precepts and the conventions. Those who seek to obey nature, through the discoveries of science, follow another set of values.

If you ask a follower of shibboleths how to overcome your troubles, his answer is consistent with his moral biases. Should you consult a devotee of science, he gives you conclusions built on his insight. The solutions of the latter seem selfish to the former.

The compromisers see nothing evil in defiling personality just as savages thought it right to distort their bodies. To those who believe such deformities are wrong, NO COMPROMISE is a basic tenet of integrity. To become a sickly *halfway man* seems inexcusable.

Faced with this division, the question of living life well is not one of wisdom only, but of daring. You may have intelligence enough to see a practical solution. Have you the nerve to follow it? If not, you might as well be stupid.

There is no right and wrong for you, therefore, in the handling of your problems until you decide what you mean by right: either adherence to the stereotype, or obedience to cosmic law. The first step we must take in any discussion of overcoming life's difficulties is so to clarify the consequences of the various procedures possible that we come to a definite decision as to where we stand.

There is power in conviction. If you believe you have the forces of truth on your side, you have the strength of ten. If you doubt your decisions, the greatest wisdom is forceless. This is a point consistently ignored by books on the art of living. They characteristically give you convenient little recipes for happiness, which cause you pain when followed, unless your heart is friendly with your head. You cannot imagine Mrs. Saisis following the best methods for meeting her parental and marital crises if that wisdom was against her biases.

It is for this reason that advice is never practical unless it arouses faith. Belief is essential. Without it, the battle is transferred from circumstance to a man's breast. His soul is torn between two wills, neither of which he can follow with confidence.

If I had only a few central points to offer for overcoming our daily quandaries, the first would be: "Don't follow any advice, no matter how good, until you feel as deeply in your spirit as you think in your mind that the counsel is wise."

And the second caution would be like the first: "Don't assume that the established ways of thinking about human conduct are true and perfect just because they are established. They are quite as likely to be as insane as the customs you repudiate."

The Better Laziness

As the taxi sped him from the station, Elwood Winters smiled ruefully. He would soon be at the scene where he had spent years of effort, back at the task to which he had given his youth.

He found the new manager, Farnsworth, sitting comfortably in his office smoking meditatively. He had lots of time to himself, he explained, lots of time at a task that had driven Winters from morning to night.

"How do you do it?" Elwood asked.

"I never do anything I can get someone to do for me, and I don't touch a task myself if I can get some method or some instrument to do the work. We're living in a mechanical age. We don't paddle across the ocean, or dig ditches with our hands. We use tools. I make mental tools do my work."

"What sort of instruments and methods manage this company?" Winters demanded incredulously, thinking of the strikes and sabotage that had caused his collapse.

"Three of them," Farnsworth smiled. "One method, and two instruments. First, I found it was necessary to get more morale into the men. I formed a promotion committee and left the question of advancement in their hands. Then I imported the council method we'd had at school. You went there, too. Wasn't there a student council in charge of all discipline?"

"Why, yes, certainly."

"Well, I've employed exactly the same method here, and it works. They are more severe too than I'd be, but the men take it from each other. Thirdly, I've an experimental department for business advancement. It concerns every branch of our work. Each employee spends one day a month there. He has a chance to see the whole problem of the business as it relates to his work. He's offered a bonus for every suggestion he can make. He's paid for any invention he originates and compensated for formulas, sales and advertising hints as well.

"The men like the creative spirit this research offers and rise eagerly to the competitive opportunity. We've improved sales and gotten no end of good ideas. But the best of it is, the men see what our manufacturing and selling job is. I merely direct things now. They manage themselves. In fact, I've decided to keep away from the plant more than I did at first. A fresh perspective is quite as important as a lot of effort. And after all, there's always a method. Say, do you remember me back at school?"

Winters nodded. He had not thought it wise to bring the matter up, for Farnsworth had been a problem to the very student council he now so admired.

"I get the cause of your reticence," Farnsworth grinned. "I sure was a case in those days. I wonder if you recall Sudbury, our English teacher. He was my counsel for defense in a court-martial once, and the way he saved me from dismissal has always stuck in my mind.

"I'd done all the things I was accused of, and I hadn't a chance to win in that hard-boiled court. It was one of those grand spring days we get down South sometimes, and I looked around the campus at the other cadets, wondering what Father would do to me when I got home. Sudbury seemed calm enough, however, about my case, and spoke confidently of my continuance at the school. 'There's always a way to win, my boy,' he smiled, 'and I want you here. There are some things I need to teach you.'

"I stayed too. His method was as simple as the hills. He surprised the court by making no defense at all. I was the only witness. He put me on the stand and made me admit every charge against me. My case didn't involve anyone else and I told it all. Then Sudbury rose: 'Gentlemen of the court, you have had a superb example of frankness, integrity and good sportsmanship,' he said in his gentlest tones. 'The defendant proves by his sincerity that he is a clean, honest American boy, caught in the natural mischief we expect to deal with in every school. This Academy publicly announces that it can take any boy of character and make a man of him. If it is the will of the court that he be dismissed, we would certainly owe an apology to his parents and a withdrawal of our word to the American public.'

"They couldn't drop me after that, of course. Sudbury had merely taken the school's boast on its face value and used it word for word in my defense. They couldn't have sent a report of that court-martial to my father on a bet. He's a lawyer, you know, and he'd have caught Sudbury's logic on the instant.

"I learned a lot at the Academy after that, but the most important thing of all was the fact that there's always a method or an instrument that will work for you and save you trouble."

On his way back to the station, Winters thought of the recent months at the sanitarium and what they had cost. He counted up the salary he would have received. And all because he had tried too hard. Some might think that faithful effort didn't pay. And it didn't as he had done it. But that wasn't the real truth of the matter. He knew that now. It was HOW he had worked that had failed. Loyal toil could be expended endlessly and never be appreciated if he didn't do it the right way. Well, he'd learned a lesson. He'd handle his new job very differently—thanks to Farnsworth.

A journey across a continent was once arduous. Nobody made it so. Man, through science, has conquered this dilemma of distance. Making a yard of cotton cloth used to be an endless task. It has been turned by man into a simple matter through the invention of automatic machinery.

Success in handling problems consists in gaining the attitude of mechanics and of learning how to harness one's selfishness in relation to social requirements so that the dilemmas of life are constantly overcome.

It is the purpose of effort to discover the better way. To lift a mighty rock from a field of loam would strain a giant's back. To pry it loose with a crowbar is not difficult. To make a hole deep in the earth that water or oil might be extracted from beneath the soil once took years. We bore it now with a drill, swiftly and with ease.

Every act of conquest in nature has been achieved by the use of methods and instruments. In the objective realm we take this fact as a matter of course. In personal problems and subjective anxieties, we neglect to follow the same principle. We not only fail to look for such keys, but we contest the idea that they are available. Just as our forefathers opposed each mechanical advance, deriding those who supposed the "hard facts of life" could ever be conquered, so we refuse to believe that the control of circumstance lies largely in our attitude toward it.

It matters little whether yours are the dilemmas of love and mine money anxieties, or the problems of food, clothing and shelter. The question of how we deal with them is all important. It is we, with all our personal uncertainties, who are caught in the mystery of experience, we who seek understanding and an opportunity to overcome the odds against us. While we pray for money to pay the bills, there should be supplications for insight to stimulate our wealth-producing abilities.

Money is made by men whose minds are free of muddle-headedness. Power and plenty, position and even pleasure do not come with any permanence as long as constrictions of consciousness create mental compromise.

He who has not means and seeks them, she whose independence and ease are conspicuous by their absence, need to put their lives in order that their wits may work on the winning of affluence. No frenzied focus on objective tasks will force life to give us good fortune if we continually circumvent favorable events by mental obliqueness.

It is part of life to overcome, and again to overcome, whatever hinders us. Fortune changes when we change. He who puts himself in order affects his relation to life in vital ways. He brings to events a new face. Until he does this, fate so seems to destroy his effort that he easily rationalizes himself as its victim.

This is why the doctrine of *never compromise yourself* is so essential to intelligent living. When you are wedged in, your power is also limited and you have a less dynamic instrument with which to overcome your problems.

How Do You Do in Trouble?

The question of where you put your attention when confronted with a difficulty determines how well the problem is solved and whether or not you become the victim of the circumstance.

How do you do? When overworked, do you fuss about it, or try to reduce the strain? If bothered by inconvenience, do you stop to see how a better way can be found, or do you irritably endure the handicaps? When oppressed by your job, do you plan ways to work through it, and out of it, to a better situation; or do you fill your heart with anger? To know where you are putting your attention is far more important than to enumerate the facts of your dilemma.

To fear danger is hopeless unless you find ways to protect against it.

To dread contagions requires you to conquer the germs.

You cannot avoid loss from the carelessness of others unless you learn to control your relation to them.

When people won't let you alone, it's because you haven't learned how to make them do it.

Injustice preys upon you until you give your thought to its conquest.

Suffering is for the purpose of arousing you, teaching you, forcing you to use your wits on the problems in your life. Where you put your attention and how calmly, persistently and carefully it is directed determines your happiness. *Success begins with you.*

8   *A Way That Wins*

There is no queerer fact in life than the neglect we show toward efficiency. One would think from the way we talk that methods which succeed would interest us. They do, in theory. We like to hear about them.

In any case, Parmella Steadman observed for years the easy way in which her sister, Bernice, dominated the home. If money was to be spent on clothes, Bernice was considered first. If singing lessons were in order, Bernice received the training. When a trip to Europe was planned, it was she who went.

Ever and always Bernice was center stage. Nor was her father the only adoring worshiper of the older daughter's charms. Her mother, too, spent hours shopping with her; then weeks upon her clothing, sewing this, knitting that.

In secret, Parmella had wondered about this favoritism. And the strange part of it was, everyone took it as a matter of course. Finally Parmella had an inspiration. It came from reading a popular novel in which the heroine of the story was placed in the same situation in which the young woman found herself. The author most graciously explained not only why Parmella played so poor a second part, but gave a vivid analysis of the older sister's methods. She alternated between tantrums and flattery. The dominating vixen in the narrative paid her parents for their kindness by cooing and petting them for all they did. The shopping parties were made intriguing to the mother, the giving of presents brought a sense of power to the family provider. He was never allowed to forget how great and wonderful he was.

This adroit devotion she punctuated by fits of temper when diplomacy yielded no dividends. "How like international affairs," the author remarked, "constant secret scheming and an *'entente cordiale,'* then the threat of war, if the maneuvering failed." There was always something to adjust, something to have to decide, a strategy of affection, a hint of hate cleverly at work.

Light broke rapidly for Parmella after that. She watched her sister's skill. But what could a girl with her feelings do about it? She couldn't work her father. She loved him. She couldn't flatter her mother. It seemed insulting, as if there were no depth of feeling in their relation to one another. Yet the clever, superficial manner succeeded where hers had failed. She knew Bernice felt little devotion compared to her own.

Parmella thought patiently about her problem. There was a principle involved if she could only find it. When it came to her, she laughed at the blindness that had made it so hard. She must repay her parents. Why, of course. Not even those who loved were satisfied unless there was some reward. We are all selfish at heart. She must dedicate herself to some cause in which they would have faith, give them something to adjust to as striking and inevitable as Bernice's tantrums.

The two needs came together when she saw how she longed to enter her father's business, longed to carry some of his burdens. "I'll become his right-hand man," she told herself. "All the family treat him with consideration, is he not the great provider?"

Later, as she looked back, she smiled at the ease with which her battle had been won. It was Parmella this, and Parmella that. She was to take a business trip, having proved that as a woman buyer she was especially valuable to the firm. Mother did this, Father did that. She must not become too tired. She must dress better than anyone, the business required it.

Parmella found it easy to give a grateful affection in return for her new joy, a warmth under which her parents blossomed. She had discovered at least one key to conquest.

When Parmella married, it brought new problems. As the years passed, her husband became critical. He turned his faultfinding on her handling of the children. Nothing she did seemed to satisfy. Her unhappiness over the situation lasted until she decided there must be some conquering conduct not less efficient in this new dilemma than the means she had used to win her way through her family quandary. Was she really so inefficient? she wondered.

To discover the facts, Parmella imported into her marriage difficulty the orderly methods that business life had taught her. In her journal she kept a record of the day, reporting the situations and remarks of her husband when his blame of her flared up. Then quite as if by accident, and in a gentle manner, she withdrew from each responsibility he had found her incapable of handling.

"You take care of the matter," she told him. "I'm certainly no good in dealing with it."

When Conrad did no better, and often worse than she had done, she put her report on the proper page close to the outline of the difficulty. The time soon came when he exploded. He could not be bothered with all these nignags, he told her. They weren't in his line.

"I think you're right, Con. They aren't in your line. Then why don't you leave them to me?"

"I do when you let me," he contended.

"Do you, dear? Will you read this little journal? It's dated and right up to the minute. And it won't take you long."

It didn't. It took an even shorter time for Conrad to see just what had happened, to face unavoidably his own nagging.

"I *had* to make you see it, Con," Parmella explained, softly. "People fail because they don't know how to protect the truth." Con didn't answer. He merely put his arms around her and held her tight.

In every life there are turning points, little acts that mark one's stride toward success or a downward step to failure. We are constantly making these moves. Joy or pain follows inevitably. Parmella, believing she should *never compromise* herself, had dared to act with vigor in a situation that might otherwise have become overpowering. She freed herself from that half measure which so many women endure in marriage.

9 *No Ego Satisfactions*

Horace Headlison read the letter again. Politely, but firmly, it asked him to submit his resignation. There was nothing new about that for Horace. He was always in trouble. It wasn't limited to his educational activities. Few would deny he was a brilliant teacher, so capable, in fact, that some school always stood ready to employ him no matter how many times he came into collision with executive heads.

"It's just as bad among our friends—you know that, Horace," his wife told him. "You've quarreled with the Asburys and offended the Witherbys. Mother won't visit us now, after the way you've talked. I'm tired of being criticized and blamed. You justify every mistake you make and find me responsible for most of them."

Had Helen the right of it? Horace wondered. There'd been justice on his side, a justice no one was willing to see. Grimly he went over his life since school days. It was a series of quarrels. But he'd fought for good causes! He'd been in the right mostly, and had had the satisfaction of hearing that the ideas he'd contended for were put into effect after he'd left. He'd been right, too, in relation to their friends and his mother-in-law. He'd only seen plain facts, said what needed to be said.

Was that all of it? Again Horace wondered. Did he like it when others came at him as bluntly as he sometimes spoke? Didn't their arrogance offend him? Weren't they most of the time expressing themselves, not caring much for the cause they argued for? Some of them got away with it. His father, now; he'd ridden rough-shod over everyone for years, telling people just what he thought and always having his own way.

Horace brooded bitterly about the old gentleman's asperity. He was a martinet. Now, if Helen had married a man like that! But suppose she had! She'd at least have known what to expect. Horace Headlison, Senior, left no one in doubt as to where he stood.

A glimmer of light broke into the younger man's mind. His father was a consistent dominator. He put all his power into being an efficient egotist. His word, his will, was law. He intended it should be. He ran his business that way. Fear held his men subservient. He'd run his home that way. Not a child had gone against him.

There'd been no marriage contest in that house. Mrs. Headlison worshiped her husband's will. So that was the secret of it, thought Horace. One could say what he chose and have his purposes carried out if he became an entrenched autocrat. He'd been a *halfway man* all his life.

But wasn't there something more to it? Understanding was forming in the educator's mind. He recalled something Pestalozzi had said about no one being able to teach anyone by telling him what he ought to do; that people should help others to *discover* truths, not *assert* them. That, too, had been his mistake. If he'd surrendered his ego to the purposes he'd thought he cared about, and kept his pride out of the conflict, there wouldn't have been any such upsets.

He recalled struggles in which he'd had his say and lost. Yes, it wasn't his honesty that brought ruin. He'd tried to put ideas over by the force of his will. It hadn't worked. But must he become a subservient and tactful follower of others, indifferent to the outcome, or could he learn to surrender his personality to the good purposes? He must, because—and Horace laughed as he thought about it—he wasn't a consistent martinet.

So it is with each of us. If you don't wish to be a tyrant in home and factory, if you aren't brutal enough to become a dominator, yet would hate to be a helpless underling, you must learn the art of *no ego satisfactions*, surrendering your pride to a passionate seeking for natural decisions and cooperative actions. In mutual aid lies the key to happiness. Power rules, but love wins. This is true no matter how small your disputes, how casual the trouble in home, office, and at social gatherings.

Solutions to the riddles of intimacy are not difficult, are in fact simple to understand and easy to apply, if —and this is a great if—you are willing to apply them. Surrender to law is the answer. No one who cares more for self-glory than for self-expansion is concerned with meeting life successfully.

Just as the *basic law of selfhood* determines success in general conduct, so the MAGIC FORMULA unlocks the riddle of human relations. Never let your attention be deflected by emotionalized incidentals, or fixed on neurotic consequentials. Keep your problems objective. Don't identify with them. Don't become involved or personal. Treat them as an interesting experience and do what you can in each new adventure.

Let us suppose that you are in a serious quandary. You, too, let us say, have received a peremptory letter from your employer. It makes you angry. You would like to tell him just what you think of him for putting you on the spot. What will the outcome be? You will lose your job.

Do you want to lose it? Probably not. If your purpose is to keep it, you must straighten out the situation. You will try to do this without upsetting your relation to your boss. If you wish this more than you do giving him a piece of your mind, you will talk to him without furor.

Or suppose you are a woman and your husband has left you. A divorce has become inevitable. There are family matters to adjust. You would like to punish him for his conduct, even though you long ago realized you had made a great mistake in marrying him. What ends do you want to accomplish in your talks with him? Do you wish to make an agony of the sad situation, to feel that the years of association are soiled and ugly? Then you will vent your spleen,

But if you consider the children and the families of both of you, if you want to keep the respect and friendship of the man who has lived with you so intimately, you will avoid that fearful mistake of "the woman scorned," and act with decency.

The principle of *no ego satisfactions,* when the action would be ruthless and crude, touches every aspect of life. You are upset about your boy's behavior. What change do you wish to bring to pass? You can antagonize him by punishment, lose his respect by hysterical nagging, make him secretly hate you by abasing him, drive him to worse conduct by coercing him, or win better behavior by loving understanding and gentle explanations.

This does not mean that you indulge in a sentimental compromise of your integrity for the "good" of your son, but merely that you *adjust your action to the end in view.*

One of the advantages in understanding constructive selfishness lies in the protection it gives us from that smirking self-sacrifice that so infects our human relations. If there is anything more unappetizing than unselfishness done as a duty, anything more nasty than the ways of coercive goodness, philosophers have yet to find it. That good old Anglo-Saxon word "stink" is not supposed to enter polite society. Anemic members of our emasculate culture think the word vulgar. It is needed to describe the odor of sanctity that goes with self-complacent unselfishness. High in the art of living comes the wisdom of never letting anyone do anything for you until he is so anxious to do it that you know he is doing it with real joy.

Most people have the wrong attitude about cooperation. They believe that when doing something with another, one must adjust to the other person's peculiarities. Some measure of this adaptation is necessary; but when it is the only purpose, failure and irritation follow. *No ego likes to bend to another's pride, nor is this cooperation.* You should yield to the needs of the situation, but you must insist that your companion do the same.

If we cooperate in rowing a boat after a shipwreck, it is the exigency of the storm and the art of navigation to which we must adjust. We yield to the needs of the hour. If we cooperate when dancing, it is the rhythm of the music and the measures of the dance to which we give ourselves. If both have this aim, there is little need of subservience to one another.

10 *A New Golden Rule*

Jasper Judson closed his eyes as if to shut some painful picture from his memory. He was a wizened little man, whose nervous hands picked at the upholstery. Weariness and despair brooded in his voice.

"Frank was always my favorite," he said at last, "and I did everything for him. I'd not had many opportunities when I was a boy but I certainly gave them to him."

"What did you do for him?" I asked, certain of what I would hear.

Judson seemed hardly to hear my question. "I'd grown up in a mill town, and had to work, part time, when I was six. I got some schooling, but after I was twelve Mother needed all I could earn. It wasn't so bad. I liked work. But I wanted to study, too. I used to sit at my books till long after midnight. That's how I got on—worked days, learned nights."

"When did you play?" My voice was low to diminish an explosive response.

"Play!" My attempt to soften the discharge had done no good. "Play!" he repeated. "I didn't play."

"So you wanted to give Frank a chance to do so?" I queried, as if the idea was most obvious.

"No," he shouted. "No. I gave him the things I'd missed. When he was three, I got him a nurse. She was

43

a good woman. Grew up to the north of here, and had an exemplary father. She taught him his letters."

"Was she yellow?" I demanded unexpectedly.

"Yellow?"

"Yes. Shrunken and yellow, wrinkled, thin-lipped, pale gray eyes, iron gray hair, sort of sharp nose, long, thin hands, spoke precisely?"

"Did you know her?" he asked incredulously.

"Yes," I mused, "I knew fifty-seven of her. She was good at grammar and arithmetic."

"Splendid," he agreed with enthusiasm.

"And had a good idea of discipline?"

"Say, she could have run an army." His ardor was mounting.

"Why did you give her up?"

"I didn't. She became our housekeeper. We lived a good, sparse life. Miss Flint used to read to Frank from the time he was four. I selected his books most carefully. He had the best clothes: nice white collars, and the prettiest little hats. She bought them. Said she'd never had nice, lacy things herself, and it was a pleasure to see how she could dress him up. In the summer she took him on long walks, and sometimes went to the city to see the museums. I sent him to a military academy when he was twelve."

"What did he do summers?"

"I took him into my plant so he could get the discipline. Work's the best thing for a boy. But I didn't want him to struggle as I did, so I put him in the charge of my best foreman. McIntosh could teach anyone, he could."

"I see. You practiced the Golden Rule from start to finish, doing unto Frank as you would be done by."

"I certainly did."

"I'm sure of it," I agreed with sudden emphasis. "And now you tell me he's gone wild."

My companion's face changed. His eyes narrowed.

"He's been drinking. He's run off with a lewd woman, and he's in with that Greenwich Village gang. Unfortunately, my partner, Thompson, always loved the boy. Left him a bit of money. And he's going through it like water—late nights, dances, theaters."

"Yes, he would, of course," I mused quietly, "but he's not a bad fellow."

"Not bad! How do you know?"

"You asked me to see him when you wrote to me."

"And you did?"

I nodded. "He's quite different from his father. How did you expect him to like the things you liked?"

"I obeyed the Golden—"

"Oh yes, yes," I interrupted. "That maddest, saddest, most terrible rule, as millions interpret it. That maker of hell on earth, as they used it to justify their egotism."

I passed him a book as I spoke: a treatise on the old masters, full of reproductions and stories of their love escapades.

"What's this for?" he puzzled, thumbing the pages.

"It's a fascinating record of the artists. I thought you might like to borrow it. And this book of modern plays. It's an omnibus, you know, all the best things the Guild has done."

"I haven't time for such nonsense," he growled.

"No? Now, I adore it. I thought you'd want to read it."

"Say, what are you driving at?"

"Trying to show you that your boy has gone wild because of the Golden Rule. You have done unto him as you were done by. I was offering to loan you these books, and doing as I'd been done by. You hate them. Your boy hated everything you did for him. The Golden Rule is brass, or base lead—no, not even lead."

"You say that?"

"Surely I do. It sends boys and girls to the dogs. It's sent millions there. Anything that does that is worse than lead. Lead has some use; the Golden Rule, in your hands, is a grim jail of iron bars, a very convenient means of dominating others, and of working your will upon them. There never was anything more evil than that."

"What would you substitute?" he asked, too shocked to protest. "How should I have treated my boy?"

"As a first step, you might learn to do unto others as they would be done by, or as you, if you had their natures, would be done by. That isn't enough, but it's a start."

"Frank wanted to waste his time playing a fiddle."

"That's what he's doing now," I nodded, "earns his living playing the violin in a dance orchestra."

"Well—" the inflection in Judson's voice held the horror that a Barrymore might have put into it, but I ignored the implication.

"Your boy, Mr. Judson, is musical, artistic, creative. He inherits from his mother's family. His mind is imaginative, and singularly human. He knows instinctively how people do things and why. He's a fine mimic, of voice, face and manners. Practically everything you did for him was wasted, because it was built on the pattern of your nature, not his. Your nerves make you a plodder in an unemotional routine life. Frank is sensitive and subjective. His glands intoxicate him with feeling and enthusiasm.

"As a child, he needed a chance to express himself constructively: lots of music and color, good dramas to see, adventure stories to read, boys to play with. He lacked everything necessary for his growth. I've given him an introduction to a theater man, a producer. He's had a tryout and been given a small part. He'll be a success, too, earn more money in the movies than ever you've made."

Mr. Judson sat fascinated as if some sea serpent had reared its head out of the ocean. There I was justifying his boy, and quietly condemning the father's life effort in handling him after the "good old Golden Rule." Taking advantage of the silence, I continued:

"I've seen Frank several times. He's dropped the drinking and the wild woman. He wants to succeed, now that he understands how, and he hasn't any guilt about going contrary to your desires. He has no need to show his independence by riotous living. You were the cause of his delinquencies, but he's too sorry for you now to want to hurt you."

"Sorry for me!"

"Yes, he sees all you've lost, what you've been deprived of all these years. He'd like to help you have some of the things he's missed: devotion and tenderness, you know; those rare moments of companionship when two people sit together before a fire, each understanding the other and loving the difference in their personalities. You've never had the beautiful things in intimacy. He'd like to give them to you someday."

"I hadn't time," Mr. Judson's voice was husky.

"No, you hadn't time. You worked so hard you came home as empty as a worn-out packing case. There isn't any greater selfishness, I guess, than the sort of unselfishness that works and works to give a family money, and deprives it of everything else."

In the last analysis, had Jasper Judson believed in the law of integrity, NEVER COMPROMISE YOURSELF, he would not have attempted to impose his own will upon his son. Had he believed with equal ardor in the *magic formula,* and permitted himself no ego satisfactions, he would not have used his own whims as the basis for his pseudo unselfishness. Nor would father and son have lived as halfway men, constricted by ethical ignorance.

I have examined thousands of human beings during years of clinical psychology. In my experience, the greatest single case of moral delinquency is the Golden Rule in the hands of rigidly good people.

To transfer to others the abnormal wants that control your life, assuming that what you think is good for you will be good for them, is hardly kindness. I had a relative who tried that on me in my youth. She believed in every fad, from strange foods to weirder faiths. When with her, my life, for my "own good," was restricted to that of a mad Hindu eating nuts on the rooftop of a Tibetan monastery. I was a victim of the Golden Rule.

One can't even fully apply this doctrine in terms of doing unto others as they would be done by, or as you, if you were in their fix, would be done by. I know a man who wanted to die, but was afraid to take his life. He asked his pal to kill him. The friend would certainly have wanted to die had he had the same suffering. Later on the man came out of his sadness and was glad to be alive. The desire was a mood.

Deeply seen, the new Golden Rule should read: "Do unto others as life, nature and cosmic law would have you do." Follow as truly as you can your understanding of that law, and go after every scientific means available to gain more insight. If you can't do this, at least change the old saying to include the other person's nature. In view of modern knowledge, the rigid application of unselfishness, which the old wording permitted, was evil indeed.

If you treat your wife as you would be done by, you won't consider very wisely her opposite sexual organism. You'll trespass constantly on her personal preferences. If you are a woman, and treat your husband on the basis of feminine values, you'll understand little of his masculine needs and tendencies.

When I was a child, the women in my home kept me in long curls, starched white dresses, pink ribbons, bright buckled shoes and velvet-banded, delicate straw hats.

They punished me when I climbed fences, shinned up posts, got out on roofs, chased cats, wandered in swamps, raced through thickets and shrieked when my tangled curls were combed. They loved white dresses, lace collars, fancy shoes. I was treated by the Golden Rule.

Now, I admit I couldn't wisely have been treated as I would have been done by, or as they would have been done by, had they been sturdy, self-reliant and defiant small boys. I'd have liked to have looked like a Samoan islander. I'd have acted like the son of a Fiji. I'd never have sat quietly and eaten my porridge with stately grace.

But wasn't it worse to put a little lad in the trimmings of a Victorian woman, with her timidity and frills, than to let him go nude and grow strong and natural? His way —that is, my way—was far the wiser of the two. Best of all would have been to do unto a small boy according to his basic needs, according to cosmic law, according to the ways of health and sanity. If they had borne in mind how I as a man in his fifties would have liked to have been treated as a boy, they would at least have let me be manly, in apparel as well as in behavior.

11   Know Your Own Mind

"How can I be wisely selfish if I don't understand what 'myself' is?" people ask. "I don't know what I am like."

That may be, but I doubt if the excuse is tenable. I have only to suggest to someone that he possesses faults that are conspicuously lacking to have him say: "Oh, no, I'm not like that." People know themselves, but don't know they do. Try the law of economy on your personality. Boil yourself down to a few attributes you are certain are characteristic of your nature. Accent those phases. Insist on being true to them. Don't compromise them on any occasion. From this start in personal integrity, you will soon get to know yourself.

According to modern science, you are the product of your chromosomes, those minute divisions of the reproductive cells of your ancestors that carry the psychic potentials of your ancestral lines. You, according to this teaching, are a constitution with certain endowments of vigor that determine in large measure how you act. You may have strong healthy glands, which help you to be good. You may have weak or unruly glands, making health and adjustment difficult. Your nervous poise may be stable or imbalanced.

This is neither a credit nor a fault. You may have sound or diseased organs, a vigorous or a mediocre brain, a high or a low intelligence quotient. Your abilities might be striking or poor, your possibilities great or small. That isn't your responsibility either. Emotionally, the picture is even more significant. What science calls your protopathic tendencies (in other words, the urge of your protoplasm, the motive power of your cells, the hunger drives of your being) may be riotous or orderly, surging and powerful, or mild and supine. Your instincts may press, your impulses impel; your emotions of rage, fear, sex, wonder . . . and all the feelings and sensations that go with them . . . may give you furious longings or leave you with only a mild reaction.

That, too, is nature's handiwork, created by what we call the bionomic flow, or life force, in your being. You're not to blame for what fate dealt you. Any teaching that holds you at fault because you weren't born an angel is a vicious lie.

More than this, there is no successful handling of destiny, no wise control of your troubles, until you get over any guilt about being the person you are. You must take your attention off yourself and turn it to solving your difficulties. The greater cause of failure is self-doubt, self-blame, self-consciousness; next to this is the effort to become something you aren't and can never be, just because someone or some setting demands it.

You can't get different nerves, gain somebody else's glands, or acquire his brain. You cannot command his abilities, or make yourself produce his power. Nor have you his limitations and strange mixture of tendencies. You aren't driven by the same sexual desires, nor fretted by an equal rage.

The way to meet your troubles is to cease perverting your personality and release your latent capacity. Salvation lies in repudiation of external needs and in discovering and expressing your internal nature. You cannot train a cattle dog to hunt, nor a wolfhound to herd. Each gives what science calls a "proponent response" to life. The finding of this inherent trend is essential to success in the use to which dog, or man, can be put. It is not what someone tells you you ought to do that is right to follow, but what your own organism determines.

If you put yourself in order and keep yourself so, you do not need to do more. No bogus self-coercion is necessary, no duty, other than to be yourself. The facts of your job, the requirements of your marriage, the necessities of your family, the customs of society may seem to force other things upon you. These are only delusions. *They are not responsibilities, you only think they are.* It is no more a duty for you to do them than for a hummingbird to catch fish because its young are hungry.

When you give up the tension of trying to be what you

aren't, and to do what you can't, you will do better than
your previous best. Relaxation is essential to reason,
fundamental in spiritual guidance. A nervous, high-
strung perfectionist, full of guilt because he isn't omnipotent, fumbles all he fashions, muttering when he could
speak, and leaving undone half he might have accomplished.

All in all, your constitution makes you a certain type of
being, whose rate of motion is swift or slow, regular or
spasmodic, delicate or strong. Your mind is accented on
some level of life between the most material and the most
spiritual planes. Your refinement is a matter of your
chromosomes. Your service to your fellows is a biological question.

People have often asked me: "What is the cure of
egotism?" The answer is simple: *knowledge*. Knowledge that the credit for all you are goes to life and your
ancestral stream. Knowledge that you are a reflexive organism, something of a mirror, who flashes when life
shines. Knowledge that pride is an evidence of ignorance
and silliness.

To some people there seems to be a conflict between
the doctrines of *never compromise yourself* and *no ego
satisfactions*. They cannot understand how one main-
tains individuality yet accommodates to others. They
think possession of personality implies arrogance. This is
mainly because they see so much childish egotism simu-
lating strength of character.

In fact, millions are contentious and arbitrary from the
belief that their demeanor implies strength. They fear
that good humor and a kindly manner suggest a yielding nature. Nothing could be further from the truth. Mili-
tancy makes enemies. A puffed chest and a dominating
voice invite resistance. They mark you as a weakling,
one who dares not be gentle and generous.

Good humor isn't a trait of character, however. It is

an art, which requires practice. Observe the effectiveness of persistent pleasantness. Not, of course, that suave manner of the professional persuader, or the pseudoreligious smile of the sentimentally virtuous. Heaven defend us from false cordiality, but you don't need to keep still just because an ass brays.

Most people won't believe it, but it isn't so much what you do as how you feel that puts other people at ease. We convey our true spirits in a million indirect ways: a look of eye, inflection of voice, touch of the hand. A dominant motive even affects what we don't say, or do, quite as much as it shapes our conduct.

You can't put people at ease if you don't want them to be at ease. If you are envious and full of hate, the best book on etiquette will not make you a companionable person. Interest and love for that queer creature—man —puts men at ease in your society.

The secret of being yourself successfully depends upon a wise balance, then, between the basic law of selfhood and the magic formula of intimacy. Determined to be true to your own being, you resist any compromise of self, yet never impose the ways of that self on others. You allow no ego satisfaction against the will of nature and the spirit of mutual aid.

If you wish to keep your friends and your position, never accept an honor alone. Share your recognition with all who were with you in its winning. A single credit becomes a debit. You may be the crowning stone at the crest of the pyramid, but it's the other stones which keep you there.

You aren't appreciated for all you do. In fact, if you are efficient in thought and deficient in love, you aren't appreciated at all. People prefer you to be ordinary. It makes them seem less drab by contrast.

There is a second reason why this is a successful way of life: people, while they don't want you to be too dif-

ferent, don't want you to be like themselves, or an echo of
others. To repeat their glory makes it seem insignificant.
To lose distinction in the herd makes you a dull companion. Two or three unique ways of being yourself invite
friendliness.

You can't like the individual who tries to be everything and is found everywhere doing what you would
otherwise have done, and saying what you were forced to
keep still about.

Individuality is only successful when concentrated.
There are a few ways in which you are bright. Shine
there. Keep your light for those thoughts and feelings
where you are intelligent. Retire from the discussions and
activities that are better carried on by others among your
associates. He who knows what he doesn't know and
knows enough not to seem to know it, is listened to for
what he knows.

All in all, much depends upon the art of being interesting. Put in a few words:

If you can smile and not look silly
If you can joke without being a bore
If you can laugh and keep your teeth **in**
If you can tell a good story—once
If you can listen as well as you talk
If you can work as well as loaf
If you can do whatever you claim
If you can give as well as take
And all the while keep your margin, you're—invited to
dinner.

12 *Death Takes No Holiday*

Have you ever faced death: looked right at it? Have you seen it coming, nearer and nearer? Have you felt life and all your efforts turn into the strange things they seem to one who fears his time has come? They are as nothing, the things and the situations we fight about, as nothing in the face of death.

Dr. Sampson had left only an hour before. Eric Jurgeson sat looking into the open fire. It was long after midnight, but he did not go to bed. He shuddered at the thought of it. To lie there staring at the ceiling, wide-eyed, weary, trying to solve problems that seemed to have no answers. What was the use of it? Better the comfort and the glow of the fire. That, at least, brought passing solace.

You know how he felt. You, too, have heard the hours pass. You, too, have turned and twisted through the night. Nor are you without sympathy for the mistakes Eric had made, the causes, shall we say, of the crisis in his life.

The doctor had examined his heart: "You must be careful of strain. You will drop dead suddenly if you don't have times of rest. Take more recreation, play a little."

Yes, play, thought Eric, with prices rising, taxes growing, family pressing, and even distant relatives asking what people would think if he let them depend on handouts of the welfare state. Play a little—rest! Eric rose and poked the fire.

Why should he fuss, he mused. It had always been like this, even in his boyhood. He brooded on the errands he had run and all the rest of it. He'd been handy at doing things.

Did you ever try being a comfort in the home? If you can set panes of glass, repair the roof, pull weeds, wash dishes, bandage cuts, adjust carburetors, cure sick dogs and tend babies without damaging them, you'll be busy as boy or man, busy at the twenty thousand tasks that troop into your days. You'll also be trained to meet the financial obligations that friends and neighbors find too difficult.

It isn't hard to make your house the center of a clan of dependents. I've tried it and I know. When you see someone's trouble, just cry: "Let me have it." He'll be generous in his response. Eric had been doing that until his unselfishness had worn away the vigor in his heart.

What should he do? Keep on and die? That was consistent with past conduct. Should his children be taken from their schools now instead of after his funeral?

Our medical records in America show that thousands of our businessmen have this problem, have it and fail to meet it from—But you give me the answer. Is it because they are so loving, or do they fear what people and their families will say? They are dying all around us as never before. The statistics of heart failure prove it. There must be a cause. Is it pride over "doing their duty," or fear of seeing the years that led to the crisis as equally wrong?

In any case, the problem of breaking down as a burden-bearer faces legions. It must be met. How it is met depends more upon the attitude from which we approach it than upon the facts themselves. Some prefer the wrong way. They keep on, and die, leaving greater sorrow behind them than a courageous disruption would have caused. Others believe that discretion is the better part of unselfishness.

In the distinction lies a key to the contrast between those who overcome troubles and those overcome by them. *There is no sane solution but forthright selfishness.*

We make such statements these days because statistics reveal that beyond the minor reasons for this difference, one major cause is preeminent: those who fail to overcome troubles haven't the courage to use the means to conquer them. The one who transcends his difficulties trusts his own judgment, goes into action fearlessly, and does not pause if called wicked.

Selfishness is an issue in life because it is so important a part of the solution of many problems with which we have to deal. If no one could blame you for refusing the uncomfortable duty, for giving up the wearisome task, or for leaving someone you did not love, you would not hesitate. Only because you cannot face social blame and the pride of a conscience trained to its patterns are you hindered from exerting your free will and your instinctive good sense.

It is important to our conquest of circumstances, therefore, to survey the difficulties through which we pass and to see what we believe is "right" to do. If we learn to unite the doctrine *never compromise yourself* with the edict *no ego satisfactions*, we shall do well, no matter what our dilemmas may be. Heart failures and half-measure living will then speedily diminish.

13   *How to Refuse a Request*

A little *interplay* of human relations.

Characters:
    Ross Lowman, a minister
    Alice Lowman, his wife
    Abby Lowman, his sister
    Florence Lowman, his daughter

The first scene opens in a bedroom. Ross is reading a letter. He looks at his wife over his glasses.

Ross: Dick wants me to send him another two hundred dollars. He says if I do it will carry him until he gets his store going.

ALICE: That's what he told you when he borrowed the first time.

Ross: I know, but this sounds reasonable.

ALICE: It sounded reasonable enough when he started that chicken business five years ago. He was to make a fortune and share it with you.

Ross: But Alice—

ALICE: You can't but me anymore. I'm tired of being butted. Abby buts me every time I want to do anything in my own home. And you but me when I want to get the things we need to live comfortably. I slave and save so you can send money to every penniless member of your family. But I won't any longer. I'll run up bills on every charge account I have.

58

Ross: But Alice—

Alice: Don't but me, I tell you.

Ross: But Alice—I want to explain. I—

The door slams and then Ross begins to think. Was there any earthly reason why he should continue to let Dick work him? They were cousins, of course, but did it follow that the blood relation could be traded on forever? It was different with Abby. She was a sister, and a woman. But was it different? Abby was a trained stenographer and quite able to work. It hurt her pride to take a "menial position" as she called it. Was it so bad? She hadn't been much expense, of course, and no bother—at least Ross felt she wasn't much trouble. He—

The door opened and Florence, his daughter, burst in, crying: Aunt Abby stopped me from practicing, Dad. She said she had a headache and couldn't bear it. She's had something wrong with her every day this week. I'll never get anywhere if I don't practice.

Ross: But Florence—

Florence: Oh, I know what you're going to say. I should try to be more patient. I've waited for three years I've never had any freedom since she's been here.

Ross: But Florence—you should—

Florence: Yes, but I won't. You've told me to consider her until I'm sick of it.

Ross: But you should love—

Florence: No, I shouldn't; not when you push her down my throat. I hate her.

Not until that moment had Ross Lowman discovered that his wife was standing in the doorway, and his sister cowering in the hall not ten feet beyond her. Both women must have heard everything Florence had said.

Ross: Do you allow your daughter to speak to her aunt like that, Alice?

Alice: Yes, I do. I'm proud of her. I wish I'd had

her spunk. But I will now. Abby can leave—this week—
or Florence and I will. And if we do, we won't come
back.

ROSS: But Alice—my parishioners. What would they
think?

The figure in the hall stepped forward.

ABBY: So that's all you think of me, Ross. I stay just
to save your reputation. Well, I'm going, and I'm going now.

The second scene opens in a bedroom. Ross is reading a letter. He looks at his wife over his glasses.

ROSS: I have a letter from Abby.

ALICE: Ye-e-s?

Her voice rises in a tone of immense indifference.

ROSS: She sends you her love.

ALICE: Ye-e-s?

ROSS: And her gratitude.

ALICE (*sharply*): What for?

ROSS: For getting her to leave here and support herself. She's to be married.

ALICE: Really?

ROSS: Yes, and she says it would never have happened if she'd stayed here. She has your idea of unselfishness now. She thinks I was being selfish when I
let her stay here so long.

ALICE: You were. It wasn't love for Abby; it was
fear of your parish.

ROSS: You still believe that?

ALICE: Don't you? Honestly now, dear, isn't it true,
and wasn't it far better that Abby went?

ROSS (*slowly*): Yes—yes, I guess it was.

And one might add: it nearly always is. One of the
greatest selfishnesses we discover is the supporting of
timid relatives, in and out of the home, enlarging one's

ego in secret by keeping them in a parasitical condition. Thousands of children are sacrificed on the altar of duty to aunts and uncles, brothers and sisters, cousins and predatory friends. Sometimes the "heathen" are fed while malnutrition more serious goes on in the home. And all this in the name of virtue. Besides, rarely is the persecution of the young of any benefit to the ones who exploit them. Abby might have ruined Florence's future, but it would also have hurt Abby.

What is not good and constructive for every member of a family is not good for any member of a family. Self-denial to support those who *claim* they cannot take care of themselves in the end injures the one supported. Life is for growth, not to pamper the ego in indolence.

We need to shake up this question of blood kin, and to shake it up well. As now constituted, it is a disease-producing and dreadful tradition, causing agony, hardship and often death.

If Christianity is founded on the teachings of Jesus, one might well question if Ross Lowman had any more right than you or I to let relatives become predatory creatures. There are many who don't know their religion as well as they know their traditions who will disagree with such healthful doctrine. But they are only justifying their own inadequacy by rushing to tell you what you "ought" to do in your domestic problems.

This is one of the worst forms of selfishness. It is one of the reasons why the seemingly virtuous are so often evil. They are the ones who prate of duty, and yet their own is done with such hateful and smirking complacence.

No one but yourself knows what you ought to do. You discover it when you no longer fear condemnation. *Nothing becomes an obligation merely because someone tells you it is.* This being the case, there is only one way to refuse a request with a clear conscience: decide what relation to life the request bears. Refuse to do what anyone asks if you do it only to please him. Refuse with equal fortitude to endure any situation unless you see it as a cosmic responsibility.

Through the years of my practice, I have received many letters like the following:

"My life is made a torture by quarrelsome relatives in my home. They waste my money, my strength and my time. My mother tells me it is my duty to take care of my blood kin. They are good-for-nothing and lazy. Is it necessary for me to support them?"

The answer is: No. *Keep the world off your back.* You don't have to carry it; you only think you do. If you start to pay toll for the privilege of living and accept the pressure of everyone who creates it, you will be broken indeed. The world is full of people who wish to live like beggars. If you accept the doctrine of standing on your own feet, insist on giving others the same privilege. Every time you carry a healthy person, you weaken him.

We hate to name those who upset us. It seems disloyal. But is it? One day we will hate those we claim to love if we let them prey upon our lives. It's kinder to be honest in the first place. Hating someone and feeling guilty is about as foolish as loving someone and feeling virtuous. God made love and hate; you didn't. They are sentiments that rise in you from depths beyond any power of yours to change.

And anyway, you can't continue to love greedy relatives, for those who trade on the blood relation always drive sharp bargains. The cheat is not more prevalent in the market place than in the home. Beware of the tricks of those who put "family" above fair play. Their affection is counterfeit.

The tyranny of the weakest member of a household is worse than its strongest egotist. A sinkhole isn't as vigorous, but it's more dangerous than a cliff. Don't let dolorous despots ruin your life just because they are timorous. What they need is trouble and plenty of it.

Duty is a state of mind. It is something about which you have a belief, just as people once believed it sinful to have bodies. Your duties change with your growth of understanding. They are fixed only by your comprehension of them. The artist, Whistler, once remarked that a great painting was made by knowing what not to put upon a canvas. Successful living depends upon knowing what not to do. He who realized when to say "*No!*" and can say it pleasantly and without embarrassment, has won half his battles.

When you come to the point where you've decided what you think is right and don't intend to change, say so calmly, but with such finality that it is quite evident to others.

Shortcuts in human dilemmas:

If you won't—if it's a fact that you won't—learn to say so in just two words, and stick to them.

If you have a difficult letter to write, try to express it in ten words.

When pressed, send an exact duplicate of the first letter as many times as necessary.

To close your eyes and sit still is an excellent answer when all else fails.

A steady gaze—at the other man's lips—is golden speech.

"I wouldn't think of disagreeing with you for worlds."

Never assume a responsibility you can't see through, and when you refuse, be firm. It saves trouble for everyone. It's better to precipitate a crisis in the beginning than to have it in the end. Keep your independence even when you've made a promise. If you have agreed to something unwise, don't be a literalist and assume you should carry it out to the letter. *You have a right to change your mind*.

A promise is a vow not at all dissimilar to that made by the worshiping peasant at his shrine. It is made to God, to life, or to oneself—take it as you will. It is not made to anyone else, no matter how worded. It retains its vitality only if it is good. If I were a cannibal and promised to kill a fellow creature and bring him to you that we might eat him together, I would keep my word—unless I discovered that such killing was evil. Then my word is taken from me. I have not broken my promise to you. Life has removed it. This is equally true of every promise.

There is a very good rule about doing a favor. Don't do it unless you can give whatever the favor required without expecting anything in return—even adequate thanks. Some things are a matter of give and take. A favor isn't; it's a case of you give, they take. Either let them have what you contribute of time and consideration, or admit you are not generous enough to stand the test. There is nothing more disappointing than to anticipate a reward for kindness. Somehow it leaks out when you expect gratitude, and changes a blessing into a barter.

In other words, in this question of refusing a request, you do not merely consider yourself or the other person, but seek to apply the spirit of mutual aid on a truly cooperative basis. When a request is an imposition, it trespasses on one's basic right *never to compromise oneself*. Nor should one do a favor self-indulgently as a *mere ego satisfaction*. Only when life is constructively flung forward, both for you and for the one you help, is such a service wise.

14   *Is Self-Protection Right?*

I met him on a steamer: one of those splendid boats that
run from quaint Victoria to Seattle. He was taking a little vacation, recovering from strain. He had, you see,
been married twenty years. You'll admit that that's a
long time. It's longer if your wife is a hypochondriac,
who keeps the household on the jump: opening and shutting windows, cooking special meals, running for medicine and doing a thousand other things that a bedridden
woman can think up for others to do.

My companion told me his story while we coasted
along under the great Olympics, and now and then
scanned the lovely head of old Mount Baker to the east
of us. His wife, it appeared, also had a martyr complex.
She was sensitive, cried at the least suggestion of unkindness and was especially upset if her father's ways were
not carried out just as he would have wished them done.
It gave her hysterics when her husband hinted he might
not vote the Republican ticket. "Father, were he alive,
would have been so upset." And as for not going to his
church, it was unthinkable. Mrs. Barnaby didn't go herself, but then she couldn't. Stephen went for her.

One after another the symptoms of hysterical domination, the wild will of an enthroned child, occupying the
worn body of a nervous woman, and fixed on the memory of an adored parent, came to light. Mrs. Barnaby
had taken to her bed when her father died, and never gotten up again.

You'll admit that Stephen had a fair-sized difficulty.

"I've never found anything that could help her," the weary man complained.

"But she's not the one who needs help," I answered briskly.

"Why—who is?"

"You are."

"I am? I'm not sick."

"Yes you are."

"What with?"

"Fear. Fear of the consequences if you should dare to get out of your awful prison. Fear of consequences if you should stop being a cowardly slave under your wife's despotism. You are afraid of using the means to cure her."

Mr. Barnaby looked at me as if he were hearing heresy, but he wanted more.

"How could she be cured?"

"Has your family doctor horse sense?" I cut in.

"I don't know. He's said something several times along your line of reasoning."

"And you've refused to listen."

"I guess you might put it that way."

"All right. Then here's your answer. First, since you come from New York, I'd send you to this dramatic school to learn to act." I passed him an address as I spoke. "I'd get them to teach you how to have tantrums, to outplay Lady Macbeth at hysterics. Then I'd choose a convenient time and have you become sick. I'd have you lie in bed and be fuller of whims and whams than Mrs. Barnaby ever dreamed of. Your mother is living, you tell me. I'd have you send for her and get her to stay in your home as long as—well, until your wife got out of bed. I'd take your doctor into your confidence and have him very much in evidence. With his help and your mother's co-operation, I'd put that house of yours into such a whirl your wife would prefer the merry-go-round at the circus as a resting place."

We talked a while longer, as I added artistic touches to the program. Mr. Barnaby listened, but said nothing. After we turned into Puget Sound, a friend joined us and the discussion ceased.

It was five years before I saw my acquaintance again. He looked the picture of health. His wife was with him: a pleasant little lady, who seemed eager to go with him everywhere. They were planning a camping trip into Canada. I couldn't see much evidence of the invalid I had imagined her to be.

After a while, Mrs. Barnaby joined a group of ladies and her husband had a chance to talk. He held out his hand:

"We shook when meeting, but I want to thank you for that advice you gave me five years ago. It worked, as you see."

"You applied it, then?"

"Yes, to the letter. My doctor was enthusiastic over the idea, said my wife wasn't really sick, only hysterical and self-indulgent. Anyway, he agreed. So I went to that dramatic school, and I did learn how to act, and especially how to have an hysterical spasm. I worked all winter at it. Then I took the next summer's vacation in bed. I was tired anyway. Mother came on and my doctor saw her. I guess she liked the plan too. The doctor suggested I'd have to give up business unless we sold the house and took a smaller place. We sold it too, but not until my wife and I had been sent to a rest ranch in Arizona.

"Freda stood it there for three days, and it was pretty rough. Then she packed up and went East alone. There wasn't any house to go to, so she chose an inexpensive hotel, not having money enough with her to do otherwise. The beds there weren't comfortable, so she stayed up. Meantime, I took a vacation, riding some of those western horses, and came back in the pink. I'd seen the light too, and I told Mrs. Barnaby several things—quietly, you know, and politely too. She knew what I meant. My price, now and always, of continuing to support her is that she stays up, goes where I go within reason, and keeps well. Otherwise, we go to another ranch permanently."

It's evident, of course, that unless we are to accept the compromise of goodness and truth, Mr. Barnaby had to do something to correct his situation. To have done it as a *mere ego satisfaction* would have been evil. To strike the shackles from his wife, that they might both live life happily instead of at half measure, was a way to free them from neurotic imprisonment.

15   *The Wisdom of Life*

Excerpt from a letter:

"My dilemma isn't so serious, but it's awfully aggravating and somehow I feel that the things that irritate us day by day are often more wearing than the great woes.

"My situation is this. My husband will never do anything I ask him to do. The mere fact that I want him to do it is a sufficient reason for his refusal. Some time ago, I had a great longing to go to the city for a few years, so that we could have more good music, plays and lectures. But if I suggest it to Mr. Eldridge, it would be the last thing he'd do. There isn't any reason why we couldn't go either. We rent our house here in the suburbs, and our children are married and gone. I can't see any way to bring the change to pass. I know also that my husband wouldn't mind, if he had happened to think of the plan first."

I answered this letter, and received a response from which I quote:

"I don't know whether your plan would work or not. The trouble is, it seems so selfish. I'm not a schemer. I've always been straightforward and honest. I can't bring myself to deal in duplicity."

A few months later, the good lady yielded to the temptation I had put in her way. She carried out the plan and moved to the city successfully. What did I tell her to do that shocked her so at first? Merely to use her husband's perversity to win her desire. It seemed evident that he had a mental sickness we call "contrary suggestibility." He did things by opposites, going against the wishes or influence of others. Nor was Mrs. Eldridge likely, alone and unaided, to cure him of the neurotic twist.

It became a matter then of choosing among three courses of action:

1. To continue to be the victim of a sick egotist.
2. To leave him, seeking a divorce.
3. To learn how to manage him.

The third course seemed the wiser one for a couple in their fifties. So I had suggested to Mrs. Eldridge that gently, but with increasing fervor, she speak of all the wonderful assets they quite truly had in the suburbs. I didn't suggest lying, merely a campaign of praise of the country. The facts were there. The point was to mention them until Mr. Eldridge's ego became involved in a contrary desire. It soon did. He began to hate the country. He'd take his wife to the city, whether she wanted to go or not!

Was there anything wrong in tactful diplomacy of this

kind? I've heard scores of literalists condemn it. I would condemn it too, if a woman were married to a true mate, a loving, understanding man, whose ego wasn't warped. But then there wouldn't have been any trouble to handle.

In most settings there are more egotists than altruists, more who work on contrary suggestibility than those who don't. For this reason, strategy of this sort is practical for anyone to use. Unless all your associates are happy, easy, adaptable natures, it's foolish to expect them consistently to respond to your ideas. It is wiser to approach any plan you have to suggest by first speaking of the opposite values and contradictory facts. If you believe a certain course should be taken, discuss the risks of so doing and criticize the idea. Let your listener be the one to suggest that after all such a plan is needed. Then go along with him. Most of your companions are full of pride. They like to contest suggestions. They prefer to make them. By giving them a chance to work off this personality quirk, you can put plans across.

We revere the work of a craftsman who makes a beautiful vase. Why should we not respect the man who uses his skill in the conquest of trouble? Is there anything less beautiful in a life well lived than in a work of art? Or is there anything wrong in having crafts to conquer difficulties?

After all, it is a matter of whether or not we must live life at *half* measure because of some deforming limitation in an intimate. If one believes he should never accept compromise of his basic selfhood, he cannot do less than meet his problems efficiently. The act need not be an ego satisfaction only, or an imposition of one's will upon another. It is right only when it leads to greater freedom for all.

Because evil people are schemers, is that a reason why you should use inefficient methods? Scheming is essential

to living. It is the wisdom of life. Strategy is important
to accomplishment. It is only evil when the motive is bad.

There was a certain opportunity I once wanted. I mentioned my interest in it to various friends, casually, you
know, not insistently. In less than six months a man
called me on the telephone and offered me the opening I
had desired. He happened to know three of my friends
and they had, quite unconsciously, carried out my
strategy.

Whether your ethical biases will let you believe it or not,
life is a game of chess. Fate sits on the other side of the
table watching your moves. She gives you a perfect example. If from sentimentality, you decide upon a rigidly
set series of plays, the checkmate of your plans is sure.
Make your moves according to the shifts of fortune, play
by play, but hold to your life plan as an underlying
"scheme."

Artists paint with "color schemes." Composers use
chords: tone schemes; dramatists use plots: life schemes.
You cannot overcome the odds of countless modern situations without constructive scheming. You must use it or
fail.

There is nothing more successful, for instance, than
the power of an exact equivalent. "What shall I do with
a melancholy sister?" a man writes. "Be more so than
she," I answered. "Talk and talk and talk about your
troubles. Have a fine time being desperate when with her
and see how, in a month's time, she changes her ways."
Men often fear a woman's tears. Nonsense. There is nothing in them to be afraid of. Start crying when a woman
does, and she'll stop pronto. Try it, and you'll be surprised.

Perhaps the greatest contrast between the older type
of thought and the modern advice we give is in the manner of what we call detachment. They once told you to
get down under other people's burdens, give them a sickly
sweet sympathy, get all worked up over their difficulties.

We teach you now to keep out of involvement, to have an objective and impersonal attitude. To the old school this seems unsympathetic. They cannot see that one is more helpful if his head is clear and his wits are calm.

You do picture puzzles with your hands. Then keep your difficulties out of your brain. Put them on paper. Make them as objective as the latest crossword puzzle. Seldom ponder about them if you haven't them before you on the table.

The most important strategy of all is quiet. Limit your talking to one-tenth of your doing. More effort is wasted in words than in any other folly.

16   *When Sacrifice Does Harm*

The art of selfishness consists in looking after your own needs so that no one else will have to. True unselfishness does not permit you to become a burden tomorrow, because you were saintly yesterday. Nor does it justify you when, to please yourself, you heap luxuries on others and miscall this indulgence a virtue. Scientific ethics is searching; it goes with nature, and nature in the end finds us out. See how the old ways worked in the lives of Mrs. Farwell and her son.

William was going to the dogs; there was no question about it. Since an officer from the juvenile court had come and gone, his mother could not ignore the fact. He made her see, moreover, how she had spoiled her boy.

Mrs. Farwell found it a bitter blow. When William's

father died, just as the little fellow had his first short trousers, her duty seemed clear to her. "He shall not lack anything he would have had if Tom had lived," she told herself. How she had toiled to make good her vow.

"And of course," the court officer remarked when he heard the story, "he got used to seeing you a slave, laboring that he might play. How did you expect him to learn adaptation, or to gain discipline?"

"But shouldn't I have done it?" Mrs. Farwell demanded. "I didn't want to be selfish."

"No, you shouldn't have done it. Life is greater than we are, Mrs. Farwell. When sad experience comes to a family, it is not the duty of a parent to play the part of God by standing as a bulwark against the experience. We should share life together, and learn to meet it together. You tried to be fate to your boy. He should have had to meet your loss with you. That would have made him a man."

Yes, the officer was right. Mrs. Farwell saw it now. She surveyed her bitter toil. William had never felt his father's loss, never gone without anything.

One might put this little story into almost any setting. Its principle holds between husbands and wives, even when youth is considering a duty to its elders. Assuming the role of God in the name of unselfishness causes disaster in the end.

I have kept a statistical record of this principle in examining thousands of lives. Some of my data goes back many years. The boys and girls concerned now have their own children. I find few cases of self-sacrifice such as Mrs. Farwell made that did not bring injury to pass.

Not only was the law burdened with the problem of William, but charity was troubled by his mother. Her years of effort weakened her otherwise strong body. Her worry, since the boy had reached adolescence, had ruined her nerves. The shock of his delinquency upset her glands. She herself has become a responsibility because of her "unselfishness." Must we not also consider the constructive service Mrs. Farwell might have been to others had she not become so absorbed in her offspring's temporary happiness?

She was no genius, surely, but once upon a time she had been a good neighbor and a kind friend; virtues that had disappeared when she concentrated her effort on the comforts of William. The court officer had told her that her true duty was to life, not to her boy, that only by doing her duty to life first and letting her boy share the consequences could she even do her duty to him successfully.

Such a doctrine is distinctly against the garbled ethics that has become so general since the teachings of Jesus were ignored. Our ideals are closer to those of Confucius than to Christianity, and this has been true for centuries. Have you ever studied the Madonnas of the Byzantine artists, with their constricted, stiff lines and flat masses? Something of the same semioriental perversion of the natural philosophy of the Master of Galilee still cramps our morals and encases the free-flowing power of love in confines of a ghastly utilitarianism.

Our conventions make it a virtue to debase ourselves under the weight of external duties, regardless of fitness and power. Mrs. Farwell, after all, in her quasi goodness, had compromised herself from the moment her husband died. Her spoiling of William was a mere ego satisfaction. It made her feel exalted, living at half measure and slaving for him. Like all disobedience of the *basic law of selfhood* and misapplication of the *magic formula,* her sacrifice was destined to fail before it began.

17 *Greed Is Stupid*

You have probably seen melodramas in which the character of a Joshua Enrod appeared. He was a banker in a small Midwestern city. His specialty was foreclosing mortgages on friendless widows. His face was thin, his mouth was hard, his eyes were bitter. He was lonely. No one loved him; people hated him. His greed had destroyed his happiness.

Joshua was angry. One trouble after another upset his home. First his wife fell sick. She hovered in invalidism for years, then died. Joshua had hoped to keep his daughter to brighten his old age, but she eloped. Housekeepers were hard to get. With all his money, Joshua had little peace.

He was angry, too, that his plans were so slow to develop, and his problems laggard in clearing up. He complained of endless delays. He did not know that the lag was of his making. He set a template for fate to fit, demanding that life comply with his design. Life might break him, but he would not bend. His to make the edict, destiny to comply; that had been his motto. Needless to say, the stream of events moved on, ignoring his desires.

Few solve their problems if their thought is rigid. No better way of life is possible if conceit stands in the way. Tell Enrod of a possible solution to a difficulty and he believes "it can't be done." You suppose he is eager to find the facts, but discover he means the conclusions which comply with his prejudices. All else is unsound.

As long as a man insistently fits events to the measure of his compromised personality, facts are distorted. Nor is he released from such self-centered conclusions until he is willing to free his nature from its greed.

Within yourself all events are written. You master them only within yourself. Today is a moment in your personal history. He who fumes at his troubles becomes their victim.

Millions of our citizens were given psychological tests when they were drafted. On the basis of these tests, the examiners estimated for the country as a whole such a low intelligence quotient that people rose everywhere to object. We weren't all morons, they declared. Maybe not, but when it comes to some of our ideas, we're pretty near it.

We come closest to sheer feeblemindedness in our handling of evil—greed in particular. Man has been told for centuries he ought not to be avaricious. Greed was painted as a deadly sin. In consequence, it has gone on ruling the world. If a little wisdom had entered into the handling of this predatory self-seeking, greed would by now be following man's coccyx into the limbus of antiquated forms.

Tell a man something is bad, and he's not at all sure he wants to give it up. Describe it as stupid, and he knows it's the better part of caution to listen. He never changes any behavior until he is sure it is selfish to do so.

When the old Romans discovered that "like cures like," one of the greatest laws of life appeared. The world will never be rid of greed save by the efficiency of selfishness. When men discover that evil reaps its own reward, conduct against life will disappear.

Trouble is our greatest adversary, and trouble enters our days under the protection of greed. Ask yourself this question: had cooperation and mutual aid ruled man's conduct for the last five thousand years, would your life be as hard as it now is? Think of the human assets that greed has destroyed: through war, predatory commercialism, exploitation and carelessness. Think of the cities, the works of art, the literature, the conveniences that have been annihilated. Think of the forests, the mines, the prairies that were ravaged; of the health of mind and body in the lives of toiling humanity that was disregarded.

Corruption, graft, crime and war threaten man's very life on earth. They challenge all that mechanics and science have done to strengthen and protect his position.

How was it possible for man so to commit suicide? How could humanity so destroy itself and cast away its birthright? Because of the same shortsightedness that works in your life and mine when we act within the measure of a day, a year, or the limitations of a particular experience. Let me say again, the measurement of good and evil requires the perspective of decades. We gain the little end by greed, then lose the love and confidence of those who could bring us wealth and happiness. We win the small battle and lose the whole campaign. Even millionaires lose it, by the dying of life in their souls.

If you were on an uninhabited South Sea island, most of your trouble would be simple, connected directly with food, clothing and shelter. In a pseudo civilization, you are still concerned with food, clothing and shelter, but your relation to them is indirect.

A group of militarists, for commercial ends, cause a war in Europe. Lives are thrown out of gear. Taxes are raised, food prices soar, a thousand things made difficult for you. In your neighborhood, a group of politicians put in an expensive sewer, or the trees are cut on your avenue. People, people, people everywhere, cause you disturbance. Not a tenth of your troubles are created by nature or "acts of God." Human nature is the devil in the bushes.

You may for a while be powerful enough to "keep in" with those who create the wars and prey upon the people. You may be "slick" enough at your own game. But in the end, life, man and destiny will find you out. When they discover your avarice, they then block your desires.

So, too, with any form of egotism. You yield to rage, express your mind, quarrel violently, and love is lost, a valuable contract ruined. In another setting, your feelings are hurt. You sulk, withdrawing into morbidness. Your nerves tighten, your wits become addled. In one way or another, power diminishes as arrogance grows.

It is a curious fact that greed is the outcome of egotism, or put another way, it is because of the failure of our arrogance that we turn to greed rather than less barbarous expressions of self-seeking. A man puts his confident demand upon experience and the people he feels are his rightful serfs. Time after time, fortune frowns and people fail to respond. Gradually a chance comes. The asker turns into a dominator; the taker, a conqueror. Greed becomes his ruling love.

Put in few words, greed trespasses on the law of selfhood. He who believes in no compromise of personality cannot exploit others. He accepts THE SANCTITY OF BEING as the right of everyone as well as himself. Nor can he ignore the *magic formula*, coercing others for his own ends. It is ego satisfaction that greed seeks, regardless of anything and anyone.

It is strange that, foolish as this impulse is, it has ruled the world so long. It is stranger still that while the integrity of selfishness is restrained, greed often escapes. If you speak in praise of a selfishness that returns to people a little of their birthright, you invite condemnation from many good people. But attack entrenched greed and you are called a dangerous radical. People believe, so it appears, that greed must be allowed to endure. Its predatory power seems too well protected to be attacked. But—not for long.

18   Control Your Enemies

Man is born to survive. Though his end is inevitable, there is no reason why his life can't be a long and pleasant one. There is only one thing that gets in his way. He has learned to protect himself against nature; he is gradually winning the battle against disease and time; but he has not yet learned how to defend himself against the envy, greed, malice and selfishness of other men.

Is it sinful to protect yourself against attack?

To sentimentalists, still imbued with infantile ideals, self-defense seems selfish. They would have you believe that "fighting back" is a violation of our hereditary morality (which many preach, but few practice).

Those of us who disagree with this supine spirit believe that one of the greatest duties of every living creature is to act in such a way that evil forces have less and less chance to destroy the good powers of life. If we let them run rampant, there is no hope.

The problem of enmity goes to the very core of the newer ethics. Two principles have ruled in the older philosophies. In one, you used violent means, venting your rage, satisfying your vindictiveness, conquering by fury. In the other, you allowed evil to conquer you.

Gandhi once practiced this passive method. I doubt its value to occidentals. Constructive nonresistance, however, an active campaign to overcome the enemy by positive means, is a third and middle way of dealing with evil. Let your antagonist destroy himself. Find some means of overpowering him without using force. A sort of *mental* judo or karate.

Don't fight for the sake of fighting. Don't fight to inflate your ego. Don't fight to exalt your pride. Don't fight to overcome your adversary or to punish him. Fight only to win a larger end, and fight without fighting—incongruous as that seems. Strive for the positive force, the impelling power that will be invincible in overcoming your trouble. For example, a man once threatened to beat me in order to change my mind. He meant it, too, but before he started, I said quietly: "After we are through fighting, my mind won't be changed. You can kill me, you can't convince me. You'll remember this when resting in jail." My firmness overcame his rage. We didn't fight.

I do not mean to suggest that everyone can eliminate any trouble by constructive nonresistance the first time the method is applied. If practiced until one is skillful in its handling, however, it accomplishes miracles. You seldom need to attack if you use your wits.

It has long been said that if you give a man enough rope he will hang himself. Give an enemy scope and he will cause his own failure. He'll do it by revealing some point for you to use as a checkmating factor.

A woman once had few neighbors that her husband liked, but many she was fond of. He also denied her a servant, though they could afford one. She found her housework hard. Her predicament made her sad until it occurred to her that one ill might cure another.

"Isn't it lovely," she then remarked with regularity. "I don't have to keep my house up as other women do, for we have no one to visit us and so it doesn't matter." Shocked by the slovenly condition of the place, her husband hired a housekeeper and brought the neighbors in, so determined was he not to live in a hovel.

Notice that by this method you *win by yielding*. Give up nonessentials while you strive for your purposes. Maintain your convictions, but not the petty values that hinder their consummation. Only the egotist asks a smooth path.

Franklin Delano Roosevelt knew the secret of controlling his enemies. When a balky Senator stood in the way of some vital legislation, he discovered that the Senator was a rabid stamp collector, and he used that knowledge to great advantage. One night, when he was working on his own stamp collection, FDR phoned the Senator and asked for his help. The Senator, flattered, came over that evening; they worked together for a while—and the next day, when a roll-call vote was taken on the Bill, the Senator voted for it. The lesson here is an important one. At no time during that philatelic session had either man mentioned their differences over the Bill. They had simply gotten to know each other better, and the "enemy" had become a "friend."

Sometimes an enemy is a bully—and needs no more than a show of strength to give him pause. This is as true of individuals as it is of nations. Courage and conviction are powerful weapons against an enemy who depends only on fists or guns. Animals know when you are afraid; a coward knows when you are not.

Excerpt from a letter:

"What should one do," a woman asked, "if she had a husband who refused every forward-looking thought, but put the most up-to-date machinery in his plant? Mr. Krew makes home life a torture. He treats me with the arrogant repression the ancients put upon their women. He refuses all freedom to my two daughters. He threatens to disown my son if he opposes any of his father's idea, and they all belong to the days of slavery.

"We seldom keep servants very long, for Jonas treats them like machinery and rages when they want fair pay and decent hours. It's the same in his plant. He says it's his, and he'll do as he pleases with it.

"My main interest, of course, is his conduct in the home. The way we get along now is to agree with him at once and always. But it's getting to the point where something must be done or my children's lives will be ruined. He drives every young man away that the girls bring home by his anger at their modern ideas. It's really pitiful. Is there anything you can suggest to do?"

"Yes, there is," I answered, "if you have the nerve to see it through, and have the cooperation of your three children, as your letter leads me to suppose. The power of example is of the greatest educational value, and your husband needs teaching. More than this, an explosive, dramatic and crisic experience is necessary for him. Words will do no good for a man like that. Now, what you need is to give him such a shock that he has to change his ways. So I've a plan to suggest that requires five steps:

1. Secure the complete cooperation of your children and act as a family.

2. Don't under any circumstances tell what you are doing.

3. Put the plan into excessive and constant application.

4. Make it so striking Mr. Krew wouldn't dare to tell about it or disown your son.

5. When the crisis comes, give him an ultimatum—and stay with it. If you do, you'll win.

"Now, here's the plan. Since your husband insists on the human values of antiquity, refuse any and all material conveniences that came in recent centuries. Someday while he is at business, disconnect the electric light and the telephone. Have the gas shut off and put out the furnace. Send all the modern utensils to a storage warehouse, and put the toilets out of order in your bathrooms. Serve dinner as it would have been served long ago, with the house lighted by candles and warmed by a poor grate fire. In other words, create a dramatic crisis built on your statement that there is no consistency in your husband, so you are going to give up the modern ways that are not in agreement with his antiquated ones."

"It sounded terribly radical," said a letter a week or so later, "but my daughters were all for it. So was my son. And we saw your point about being utterly thorough and firm. We cooked the evening meal ourselves on the laundry stove. We let our servant have a week's vacation, so she wouldn't be dragged in. And we eliminated every modern convenience as you suggested.

"Had you any idea what the effect of your plan would be? Mr. Krew came home in a bad mood, ready to haul us all over the coals. The house was dark and cold. He snapped on a switch. Nothing happened—still just as dark. He walked around the house and saw what we had done. The excitement began. He seemed so bewildered, then came our surprise. An explosion was due, but none appeared. Mr. Krew was too astonished. In fact he was speechless. And, you know, though we didn't mean to, all four of us lit into him at once. We told him we were through. We threatened we'd tell everyone how he had behaved. I said I would leave him if he wasn't a transformed man from that very night.

"The girls described how they'd testify in court, and Tom—that's my boy—added good touches as to the effect on his father's business. That did it. There wasn't any fight left in him. Mr. Krew just broke. I guess he was all front and pretense, poor man. Anyway, we made him sign four agreements. We'd each drawn one up, and he signed them, promising us all the independence the most modern family could expect. Mr. Krew will hold to his word, too, he's built that way. And I can't tell you how quiet and gentle he's been ever since that night—a little dazed, but acquiescent, too."

There are plenty of Mr. Krews in America; mechanically alert, morally dull. They refuse to change their minds even when they know their values are untenable. Sanctifying self-sacrifice as a virtue, they never practice it, but make it a camouflage around their ruthlessness. They then no longer see life as it is, but make facts fit their system of self-justification. This is not a deliberate deception of others, but self-hypnosis. They even suffer when they go contrary to this masquerade, becoming angry at themselves when they break some narrow pattern of self-denial. Note, however, that they do nothing to correct the situations they create.

If you deny your intellect, your judgment will go as well. Sooner or later, those whose heads are thus discarded work furiously on the details of their difficulties, but never straighten the whole of any trouble. They do their "duty" as Mr. Krew was doing his, overworking everyone on the pattern of his own virtuous denial. Unselfishness becomes thereby the soul of despotism.

Should Mrs. Krew have continued to endure her husband's egotism? Your answer depends on which school of ethics you follow.

For anyone who believed in the doctrine *never compromise yourself*, there was no alternative but to do something to meet such a crisis. The problem was to find a way that taught Mr. Krew to change his ways, yet did not lead to a *mere ego satisfaction* on the part of his family. All of them had for years been living at half measure. They faced the ruin of their lives. To strike for liberty was only another Boston Tea Party.

From my point of view, there are only two ways to handle such a despotic intimate as this, who refuses to face his mental fixities and forces them upon his family. Yield, utterly and subserviently until you die, as you soon will, or else create such an explosive scene that something has to happen. That's the best and bitterest medicine for a tyrant.

I'd add, too: don't talk, don't beg, don't argue, don't try to persuade. You only wear everyone out. Dare to precipitate a crisis and believe that the pain of it is less than that which will come if you let the agony drag on for years.

The principle of silent intent holds also when dealing with NEUROTIC SELFISHNESS: the egocentricity of the mentally sick. Their infantile vanity and immature emotionalism can never be overcome by words. Nor is the self-pity or the lash of secret cruelty which we so commonly discover in such mental states as hypersensitivity, melancholy and selfishness ever overcome by resisting it. Neurotic selfishness tries to swamp you by the way it twists everything you say into unkindness and accuses you of the very sadism it feels. Your words are elaborated, your meanings changed, evil intent is put upon you until your relationship with an egocentric has become an involved turmoil.

Drop the discussions. Give them up. The delirium of a fever is not cured by argument. Neither is the sick mind of a neurotic helped by verbal pressure. You get nowhere either by blaming such an unfortunate person for the abnormalities his early setting created. He is not responsible for the attitudes that were trained into him, nor the shocks his home setting gave. Don't abuse him because of them.

It is a mistake also to think of a person as if he were his sickness. Neurosis is as much a condition in possession of him as your own bad habits that so distort your true intent. Neither are his abnormal preferences his own, any more than your strange allergies are yours.

Decide how you would live and what you would do had you no neurotic intimates. Then live that way, regardless of the uproar. It will pass, and they will begin to get well. *Never yield to a neurosis in anyone.* Dare to oppose and ignore it.

20   *Correcting a Nuisance*

The wise man learns to send one trouble after another and let them fight it out. You know about the husband who invited all his wife's relatives to visit him so that her mother would leave.

Opposing problems, like double negatives, often cancel each other. A certain businessman had an obstreperous partner, who interfered with the running of every department. To cure the habit, he brought to the man the difficulties of the whole staff in such increasing volume that the partner could stand it no longer. From then on, he left all work but his own to the people responsible for it.

Put in a nutshell, the idea is to *win by actions; protect by counteractions.* When nothing obstructs your effort and no one blocks your way, direct methods are adequate. Few are permitted such peaceful accomplishment. The stress and strain of life come from the arrogance and ignorance of the egotists. Only by seeing their foolish actions, only by checking through counteractions, is the clutter of a futile world removed.

An officious policeman once put a ticket on my car for parking more than an hour. There was no sign at that end of the square. I walked up to the man, who stood at the crossing.

"Officer," I said, "I'm thinking of getting up an investigation into the parking problems in this town. Do you know how many feet it is from here to that one-hour-parking sign?"

"I guess it's a lot," he answered and took the ticket away.

In any case, never frighten an egotist if you wish to win. You only speed him to extra effort. A nonchalant approach is the way to handle such natures. When someone insults you, don't swell up, don't strut like a confident giant. If you think he's trying to deceive you, keep your evidences of power in the background. People take warning from our witless boasts, but overplay themselves when we appear as little targets. The worse your trouble, the less of your strength should be apparent. Only cowards shout and threaten.

You will never know the power in others if you give it no chance to express itself. Another's strength can't show if yours is running rampant. But if you reveal your needs and your weaknesses, his arrogance appears. In this way, and in this way alone, can you learn to spot destructive tendencies.

In other words, there is nothing more powerful than innocent honesty. You cannot measure your enemies when they are afraid of you. And, strangest and truest of all, the greatest protection against duplicity is sheer simplicity. When deception interferes with a man's honesty, he becomes so complex in his calculations he cannot grasp your strength. If you are as natural and ingenuous as a child, your directness puts him off. Having two faces, he cannot look in one direction. Treachery in the end destroys the wits of whoever uses it, and that is why a sly mind never knows good strategy. It cannot see beyond its own mischief. Having no conscience, it cannot understand the sturdiness of yours.

The only animal besides man who lacks the intelligence to keep still is the monkey. He also chatters before going into action. Watch a cat. She crouches. Only the tip of her tail tells of her purpose, and even her switching is unwise. Silence and sometimes a motionless waiting work a miracle. Vacuum is more powerful than wind. Use this method to do away with a nuisance by counteracting with another nuisance.

I once knew a woman with an obnoxious child. Her visits were tiresome. I had a dog, as odorous as the child was trying. He was a nuisance. I began returning the lady's child-burdened calls accompanied by my dog. Her visits stopped.

You can't, however, use this method to deal with a nuisance if it irritates you to have it in your way. The first step in its handling lies *within* yourself. Straighten out your psychic snarl. Get rid of your peeve. Fleas, mosquitoes and bill collectors are part of life. Arrogant neighbors and stupid relatives are not unusual. Accept them as you do the dirt that collects on your hands. Almost any situation can be washed up, once you become calm about it.

Make this a rule: Never attempt to clear up a bothersome situation while you are upset about it. Let it alone until the funny side of it all appears. Even a toe, sore from an April Fools' frolic of your son's, has its gayer aspects.

There are, of course, many times when the technique of constructive nonresistance is an actual "coals-of-fire" method. This is always the case in momentary enmities between intimates, whose general relationship is one of love. Your companion has become cold and aloof. If you draw away in foolish pride, it will be a long winter. Use the thawing method, overcoming the cold with heat. In other words, if you can't move an iceberg, melt it. You'll have fun doing it, too, if you accept it as an amusing task. Take some old grouch as your object—your husband, perhaps, and start in shining on him with more and more warmth. He hasn't a chance against radiant affection.

It is no use trying the "good means," however, unless your heart is loving. A smile in the right place moves a multitude. But you'll never learn to do it if you wait to face a multitude. Practice the art of good nature to discover what it is, when, why and how it is honestly felt. This is essential to an impelling sincerity. Kindness is the poorest strategy, if that's the reason you are kind. The trouble with most "success books" lies in the way they tell you what to do, but neglect to warn you that their advice will fail unless you feel sincerely what you do.

The biggest fool has something good about him, and you, no matter how virtuous, aren't a saint entirely. The art of turning an enemy into a friend lies in this fact of the good and bad in all of us. Admit to your enemy the failings he so clearly sees in you. Discover the worth in him you have ignored, and his enmity abates. We call this the philosophy of the ruling loves. If the good centers become associated with some bad ones, their positive force overcomes the evil expression. In other words, if your enemy comes to think of the good and bad together, he can't do the bad thing if the association reminds him it will injure what he loves.

I know of a boy who ran with wild companions until he realized that the diseases he might get could infect his home, and might injure his mother and sisters. The thought of them made him change his ways.

Every situation has its point that most easily gives way. *Is your enemy conceited?* Then he's overlooked a score of little things. *Is he hesitant and humble?* Then he has missed some big fact. *Is he nervous and high strung?* Then he's done something too fast. *Is he casual and confident?* Then he's too slow about something. The conviction that there is a weak spot is half of what makes you go looking for it, and the biggest factor in your finding it. Make weak-spot hunting into a habit.

Secret service agents of the great nations are taught to observe every way a new situation or person deviates from the usual, to note the bizarre and unexpected, to discover the cues to the clues. They listen for queer remarks, look for unexplained actions, watch for nervous expressions. They are alert to unpleasant or arrogant tones of voice, sudden changes of manner and evidences of secretiveness. They follow out extreme statements and watch the trends and undercurrents. That is the way to be wary and win.

Don't treat the world, however, with the skepticism you must show an egotist. You should be adroit:

Only when you are sure the other side isn't honest.

Only when you can truly remain impersonal.

Only when clever moves are also fair.

Only when you are free of pride in your skill.

Only when it is essential to keep still about your actions afterward.

Only when nature points the way, for she is most adroit of all. With what a leap has she endowed a flea. And incidentally, is the protective coloring of birds and animals dishonest? Then adroitness isn't either, on the right occasion.

When you are driven to being a strategist, be a good one, not a guilty, hesitant and half-shrewd planner. Either do it or don't. Your right to act when threatened with enmities and nuisances is, of course, limited by the laws of cooperation and mutual aid. If you believe in the edict "never compromise yourself," you cannot use any techniques that deny a constructive outlet to others. Nor will your checkmating of their evil be an ego satisfaction done for your ends merely. A wrong done to you is a wrong against life. You deal with it as such.

Here are some rules from men long skilled in mental maneuvering:

Never let your face be impassive as the orientals do. That gives you away in America. Develop a naïve, open, good-natured expression and keep it.

Enthusiasm is the best protection in any situation. Whole-heartedness is contagious. Give yourself, if you wish to get others.

When a panther is in a corner, it yawns and stretches. There's nothing more powerful than the behavior of relaxation in tense situations.

When in a predicament, laugh at yourself. Laughter is the greatest weapon in the world. Laugh until others do, but always at yourself.

If you must say anything unpleasant, speak slowly and in a gentle manner.

There's nothing so suddenly startling as a drop in your voice. A low tone is better than a clenched fist.

Never seem clever to your enemy. The bigger fool you appear, the less dangerous is his attack.

Expect egotists to be obstinate. Never suggest to them what you wish them to do. Talk of the opposite plan and let them come to your purpose.

Remember that fear is more resistant than self-will. To move a timid person, find something on the other side of the argument for him to dread, and talk about that. A ghost story drives a coward through a forest of wolves.

Never try to manage anyone else. Manage yourself and what you say and do. Maneuvering others fails. Make your mind the campaign ground of your effort.

Go toward a trouble and you frighten it. Nine-tenths of the time it is people who create your difficulties. That is why your approach to a trouble determines what happens. Seldom retreat. Go forward in the face of difficulties and the people in them step aside.

When others ignore you, they are telling you how to treat them. Every situation is full of good advice. Take counsel from the occasion and you'll know what to do.

Never trust a man who hides his stupidity. No one is bright

from morning to night. The greater a man's wisdom, the more his willingness to admit his inanities. The safest fellow in the group is he who knows his constant failures.

Fraud is an admission of weakness. Strong men play few tricks. If you don't fear a cheat, he flees in terror. Wiliness leads to witlessness. If a rogue starts by being clever, he ends by being foolish.

21 *The Higher Selfishness*

A business girl sat in a doctor's office, nervous and worn. The physician, a woman of experience, looked at her long and steadily as if to weigh the possible effect of what she had to say. Satisfied, she smiled:

"I want you to take a vacation, my dear," she said gently.

"A vacation! Why, that's impossible," the girl cried. "My firm wouldn't let me off. And besides, I haven't money enough to go anywhere."

The doctor nodded. "I know. But that's not the sort of change I'm talking about. I want you to take a vacation from being a woman. You've been working hard all day carrying the burdens of the man whose secretary you are. You've borne the pressure of his masculine ego. You clean your own apartment, get your meals and wash your underthings. And when your friends come to see you, you cook special delicacies and go to no end of trouble to give them a good time."

"But boys like it!"

"I know they do," the doctor agreed. "I'm a woman too, you see. But tell me, what would a young man do? Would he let countless little burdens be put upon him by his employer? Would he cook his own meals, wash his clothes and clean up his apartment, and most of all, would he work until after midnight to get ready to entertain you the next evening?"

"I'll say he wouldn't."

"No, of course he wouldn't. That's a woman's way. Now, I want you to take a vacation from being a woman, and every time you feel tempted, ask yourself what a young man would do, and if he wouldn't do it, you are not to either."

A story built on this little plot appeared in one of our national magazines. Fannie Kilbourne, who wrote it, heard from women from San Diego to Augusta, Maine; from Seattle to St. Augustine. They poured their gratitude upon her, and many were they who gave testimony to what had happened when this wise act of selfishness had been applied.

If I were writing a book on what young women ought to know, I'd ask to include a reprint of this well-told tale. It ought to be required reading in every home. In Miss Kilbourne's story, the heroine discovers that one of her boy friends came only to eat her food, and her boss held his job because of her efficiency. Her new protectiveness helps her to inherit the position of her superior and also to win another man's love.

In the last analysis, up to the time of receiving the doctor's advice, the heroine of this story had compromised herself, and by so doing was injuring her health. Her success dated from her refusal to continue to be misused. Her new spirit was not, however, a mere ego satisfaction, not a desire to bend others to her will. She simply refused to do anything below the level of an honest self-respect, and contested the degradation society still puts upon a woman as long as she will accept it.

A French doctor, Pierre Janet, tells us that women have hitherto achieved little fame and less power because they waste their psychic energy on thousands of unnecessary tasks. They, more than men, need to learn the art of selfishness.

Contrast if you will the absorption many of our industrialists exhibit in their work. They make it their god. Others must attend where they worship: family, friends and employees. Not otherwise is work accomplished. Consider the absorption of writers, dedicated to the production of their books. No one is allowed to disturb them while an inspiration lasts. Life must give way before the sweep of endeavor.

Or think of the flaming purpose of the Garibaldis, the Mazzinis, the Tolstois, and the concentration upon their genius of the Wagners, the Goethes and the Rodins. Is anyone allowed to interfere? People who come within reach are made to serve. Would the great music, the dramas, the statues have appeared otherwise?

Concentration is the right of everyone when dedication consecrates its purpose. Nor need we be afraid of succeeding. There are those who flee every time achievement becomes possible. They seem to feel that power and accomplishment are unspiritual, unconsciously associating failure with goodness.

There are men who dare not be assertive, women who shun their sex appeal. Unselfishness rejects such powers, you are told. Must we then live with drab women and timid little men in the name of goodness?

The higher selfishness advocates the expression of your charms and the empowering of personality. From its reaching you learn the art of human contacts, skill in being a creature of interest. Nor need these assets be gained by silly superficial correspondence lessons in "magnetism," "how to fascinate," "how to galvanize everyone's attention," "develop a hypnotic eye," "gain an invincible personality."

There is hokum enough on charm to drive anyone to a Quaker Meetinghouse. But must we abdicate the ways of winning because the charlatans have preempted our needs? Nowhere but in America could the trade in "taking ways" become so rampant. Only a land that bred the gray-dressed spinster and the thin-lipped Puritan would need lessons in lusciousness. Nor would anyone else have attempted to train salesmen in seductive methods of arrogance.

With due recognition then of the commercial sentimentalization of charm, it still remains an essential to happiness. No one will develop your personality if you don't. No one will help you to achieve response and recognition from others. You become an artist in this higher selfishness only by practice. As you learn how to touch the hearts of others, so will they yield their attention.

Nor is this a skill that is hard to master. Everyone in some secret place is lonely and craves solace for romantic needs. There is no mystery about sex appeal. Nor is there anyone who fails to seek security, or to respond to whatever you do or say connected with food, clothing and shelter. We crave position and yield to those who help us gain more place in society, who assist our orientation by broadening our sense of the familiar.

Freedom is an aim for all of us. Money means satisfaction; ways to gain it, when revealed, bind us to our mentors. Nor are we without gratitude for any and every touch of friendship, whether it be in someone's words or in his manner. If he brings us pleasure, helps us to relax and gives us comfort, we love him. If his comradeship gives a feeling of safety, helping us to avoid danger, but yields excitement and expansion, we make him a blood brother. He has helped us to be ourselves, and to express ourselves.

He who cares to offer some of these things to those he meets, becomes enthroned by steadfast love. And the magic is that gaining all, he yet takes nothing from anyone. This is why such selfishness is magical.

22   *Ways Out of Loneliness*

Caroline Fenway put away her things. It was time for Dacy's Department Store to close. Another day of drawing fashions over. A few moments later she was packed into a subway car on the way to her room. Soon her solitary meal would be over and then she would lose herself in another novel.

To have millions of people around you in a great city like New York, to have them coming, going, laughing, busy about their interests, and never have one of them look at you; was ever a desert so solitary? It made her shrink into herself the way everyone ignored her. She crept into her lonely cell like a frightened rabbit.

It had been like that for months, and she knew no way to change it. The problem of making friends and especially of knowing eligible men seemed insurmountable. What a condition to come to after four years of college life! How little it had prepared her to meet this gray agony of earning her living.

That wasn't the worst of it. There was some escape

in the evening, some solace in the excitement of reading each new romance. She could live in the joys and sorrows of one girl after another as long as the stories lasted. But afterward, in the dark, in her lonely bed, then it was terrible. Should anyone have such desires, such physical needs? She wondered.

The winter sun made patches on the floor where the curtains cast a shadow. Caroline had been sitting for an hour in the little office of Mrs. Brice, personnel manager for Dacy and Company. Just why or how she had been led to tell her story, she did not know. She was not used to talking about herself. Feverish reticence had always been her trouble.

"If you'll let me help you, I think I can get you over your self-consciousness and show you how to make friends," Mrs. Brice was saying. "As a first step, I want you to join an evening class at the art school, and give up reading those love stories. They act like drugs for a girl in your situation. Your work here at the store shows promise. I'm hoping to see you promoted to the executive branch of our advertising department. That requires you to study more drawing and color. The important thing is to get you out evenings.

"Young people make contacts when they join classes, attend churches, belong to walking clubs and go wherever others congregate. But there's more to it than that. You won't be loved if you aren't selfish enough to become a dynamic personality. How often have you heard people say: 'Oh, she's the salt of the earth, but really, you know—she bores me.' You seldom like salt without pepper, and something nourishing to go with it. I can't imagine sitting down to a meal of the white stuff. Yet plenty of people ask us to. They expect us to be thrilled by their crystal purity. I find them brackish and flee their society. And I'm only doing what anyone in his right mind does.

"Learn to forget yourself in what others are doing and saying. You must be good company with yourself to be so for anyone else. *People don't seek your society for your good, but for their own.* They may lie to you in order to make you feel like a poor serf, telling you they love you so much they want to be with you. If you believe it, you need a mental test. People make life worthwhile for you when you make life worthwhile for them. Give something vital to them and you need not fear that they will do nothing for you."

"What do you think a personnel manager is for?" Mrs. Brice asked, when later Caroline tried to thank her and tell her how she was getting on at social gatherings.

Yes, she'd cracked that problem. How queer it was that the way to become popular with men was to know how to listen to them.

"Most men are egotists," Mrs. Brice had told her. "They don't want to hear much about you; they want to talk about themselves. It's foolish to wonder what to say. Just look at them sweetly and ask questions. They want your pink ears, my dear."

It was strange, Caroline thought. How simple were the steps in successful human relations. She saw now that, being unhappy because she was lonely, she had spread her gloom about her and fretted until people fled from her. When she developed what Mrs. Brice had called the "friendship method," it changed everything.

"Human contacts are an art, my dear, and long experience with people's problems has taught me one sure lesson," the wise lady said. "Practice in a million little ways the part you wish to play in the fulfillment of your big desires, and you bring those desires to pass. It's a law of life. Learn to make successful contact with many of the girls here at the store, even if they are only behind the counters. Say a cheerful word to the news-boys, chat with your bootblack in Grand Central Station. Be outgoing on every occasion you find possible. Go into the conversation other people start. Visualize what they say. Think about it and try to feel with their emotions. Communication is the soul of human relations. You can't get anywhere in life unless you get out of your shell.

"You are inarticulate only because you are foolishly waiting for some phantasy lover to come and rescue you from your solitude. He'll never come. You'll never discover him, unless you learn how to reach into people's hearts and touch them where they live."

As long as anyone believes in compromise, he is likely to live at half measure. When his right to the love and joy he needs becomes an active demand, he finds and takes his satisfactions. This does not mean, as Caroline soon found, a theft of the satisfaction of others. Rather was it finding happiness through bringing some into the lives of those with whom she came into contact. By helping them to give up living at half measure, she filled her own cup.

23   *On Being Engaged*

A year had passed. Caroline Fenway watched the gray dawn with somber eyes. Here she was with the love she had longed for come at last. What she had believed would be her hour of radiance brought only agony. She had much victory behind her. The art class not only brought love, but the promotion Mrs. Brice had prophesied. She was happy in her work, creatively expressing herself in advertising. It wasn't painting pictures, of course. But that would come someday. Her work was going well.

Her problem now was definite. Should she marry? What would it do to her work? And to which one of the two men who seemed to adore her? Did she love either of them? Both wanted to marry her that summer and she had to admit she'd rather marry than do anything else in the world. An agony of sex pressure had long brought its temptations. Again and again she had yielded, almost satisfied a craving that would not be still.

Late that afternoon, Caroline found her way to Mrs. Brice's little office, and somewhat shamefacedly told her story.

"I'm back again," she began, "but this time not because I can't make friends. I guess—that is—you seem to have helped me too well. I really seem to be popular, and two men want to marry me."

Then she told of her dilemma and the sleepless nights fearing she would make a mistake and marry someone she didn't love. Both men, it appeared, loved her ardently.

"Aren't you fortunate?" Mrs. Brice remarked.

Caroline glanced up quickly, seeking an implication in the words, but Mrs. Brice looked at her steadily and smiled. Then she told her a story, describing a fearful motoring accident in which both men were badly hurt.

She told it so skillfully that Caroline, with clenched hands, sat there weeping. "No, no, not that, not that," she cried.

"Of course not, my dear. But don't you know which one you would go to, which one you love?"

Caroline nodded: "It's Dick."

"You see," Mrs. Brice continued, "love isn't a matter of worth of character. It doesn't depend upon brilliance or material wealth. It's a matter of compatibility. We feel a strange pull, a gravitation, shall I call it? In your case, getting over your shyness still left a little androphobia, a fear of men and of your own judgment in relation to them. You saw that Fenwick Atwood was a good man, intellectual and established. He's been a persistent and an active wooer. But Richard Strong is your man, even if he's poor and not quite so brilliant mentally. You feel his tenderness and his understanding. Your heart knows his loyalty."

"I feel safe with him," Caroline agreed.

"That's one of the surest signs," Mrs. Brice continued. "Now it would have done no good for me only to question you about the relative merits of each of these men. You'd have given me conscious-minded answers that might have deluded us both. So I had to put you through an imaginary experience that would touch your inner feeling. That's why I told you that story, placing all three of you in an automobile accident and having both men hurt."

"You told it so well, I became completely lost in it," said Caroline, "just as I used to when reading those novels. But I knew instantly I wouldn't rush to look after Fenwick. If anything should happen to Richard, I simply couldn't bear it."

"If you didn't marry him, it would be like that all your life. If you married Fenwick, you still would be living with Dick in fancy, heartbroken from wondering how he was."

"How were you wise enough to use that way to discover it?" Caroline asked.

"It wasn't wisdom, my dear, only training. We know now that in every serious problem the secret lies in knowing how to make one's thought into an experience and live in the problem as if it were an actual event in life. One needs, moreover, to meditate deeply and subjectively. By absorbing you in that story, I accomplished both ends."

If there were only one bit of advice to give for the solving of life's difficulties, it would be: Make your thinking into an experience. Make theories tangible. Put feeling into imaginary actions. *Try out your ideas by visualizing them in action.*

Caroline had had her conflict because she hadn't been deliberating deeply, but only worrying about her love tangle. She intellectualized the desirable assets of Fenwick Atwood and reasoned about Richard Strong. She hid the sex pull of her love for Dick even from herself. And more than this, Fenwick had been the ardent lover. Caroline saw now that his money gave him confidence, while Dick had been hesitant, not being sure he could ever do for Caroline all he felt she deserved.

When they think they are in love, most people, from our idiotic idea of unselfishness, are deluded by the actions of possessive affection. To be loved seems to assure them they are worth something as personalities, unselfish and virtuous in the eyes of a lover. Then they yield and marry, and you know the rest of the story. It is a commonplace.

Never marry because someone loves you. It is not an adequate reason, and sometimes a bad one. If he is possessive and jealous, he doesn't love you. He only wants you. He needs to own you to inflate his ego. Having you as a slave gives him power. If you satisfy his greed, you'll regret it all your days. Possessiveness and jealousy are signs of predatory animality, hangovers from the cave.

Marry only when the other person seems lovely to you. Marry when you love, not when you would sacrifice for him, or wish to possess him. When those twin evils, self-denial and possessiveness, enter a human relation, hell comes with them, and love flies out of the door. If you married on the basis of self-sacrifice, you would consistently pick out the poorest character on earth to wed, for that would be the greatest denial. The laws of love are, in fact, one of the proofs of the idiocy of self-denial as a way of life. To relegate your intuitive and primary desires to the background makes marriage into prostitution. To let anything but the reality and integrity of your love lead you into marriage is sheer crime.

Never step into wedlock to please another person. You defile love if you do, and if your marriage doesn't then end in divorce, it should. The true, deep drive of the mate impulse will rise someday, somewhere, to make a compromised relationship into an agony. Never let the fate of anyone else stand in the way of love, or you will come secretly to hate and destroy the person for whom you sacrificed your chance for romantic happiness. Let anyone, be it father or mother, son or daughter, and—yes—husband or wife, share with you the consequences of the coming of love into your life. Go with your love and to your love. But don't go halfheartedly, waiting until you and life are ready. Just don't start anything if you can't see it through.

Most important of all, never marry a person who can't remain a sweetheart, and with whom you wouldn't want to be, even if you didn't have the protection of marriage. There is always the danger that a man will become a husband at the expense of being a man. If he loses identity in this relationship, he will in the end lose the relation. If he becomes submerged in quasi-companionship, acting the dutiful slave because a woman dumps her problems on him, and society shoves him into the hopeless position of the burden-bearer, he'll end by being an unwanted echo.

There is one basic rule in love: "Be yourself, always." Start by being so, it's your only protection. Do nothing to win a man or woman that is contrary to yourself, for you'll only win trouble if you do. She, or he, who doesn't like you as you really are, will come to hate you secretly when the facts are discovered.

Never become an appendage to a marriage partner. Keep your native hungers, your intellectual values. Never let a man put you in the home and keep you there, or a woman tie you to the home as one chains Fido to his kennel. You belong to life first, to your partner only insofar as he or she doesn't try to possess you.

And don't forget the law of maturation. Those who marry in the twenties must wed when undeveloped in many ways, since no one is mature at that age. Both are growing. The important thing to think about is not *"What is he actually like?"* but *"What will he become? Which way is he going? How is he growing? What will he be like in twenty-five years?"*

Is he maturing your way? Will you, can you, grow together? If so, you can stay together. If you grow in opposite directions, nature will force a divorce. The evolutionary attitude is utterly essential in considering marriage. It saves you, moreover, from perfectionism. It is ridiculous to judge your prospective mate as he is, on the standard of ideals you might hope to expect in him at ninety. He cannot be as wise, tender and sympathetic at twenty-nine. It takes years to develop mellow understanding.

If your sweetheart gives promise of such unfolding, that is something. If it is your kind of unfolding, your values he holds, your psychic language he speaks, that is everything. But don't marry him if you love quiet and he adores noise; if you seek museums and he a cabaret.

You call a halt on heartaches when you face the fact
that it is better to lose love now than to wake up after
a few years of pseudo-marriage to find you never had
it.

When you compromise love, you deny and even destroy your basic relation to life. More than this, you become a block in the life of the one you marry. You take
his life by the very act of living with, or on, him. Such
self-indulgence trespasses on the basic principle of intimacy. When marriage is only an ego satisfaction,
merely getting what your whim desires at the moment,
it loses the vitality of what you seek in life.

24   *Arts of Human Appeal*

"We're facing a crisis in the company," he said, "and
my partners put the blame on me. I'm the sales manager.
But our product isn't selling."

"What have you been doing to meet your difficulty?"

"We spend all we can on advertising, and I've seen
every distributor in our field. I've used every type of
salesmanship, and I know them all, from high-powered
to alcoholic. They take our stuff, but the public won't
buy."

"What do you manufacture?" I asked.

"Candy bars to be sold at newsstands."

"And you mean the stenographers and file clerks give
your product the go-by?"

"They sure do."

"How's the price?"

"Just like the others."

"And the size?"

"Larger, if anything."

"Go get me some of your candy."

He went, returning in a little while. I took a bar in my hand. It was done up in a green oiled paper on which was printed a mass of closely written information as to the prizes to be given for a hundred of the sticky wrappers. The printing was in black and blue. The ink smelled.

"If you gave this to a monkey, he'd fling it from him," I remarked.

"That's as fine and pure as it can be made," my companion cried.

"Nevertheless, he would fling it from him."

"But why?"

"Because this green color is just that of poison weeds, or the stuff that forms on copper—poison, too. It's green-bluish, a warning of danger. And the ink smells bad. A monkey wouldn't look inside the wrapper. Neither would I. He'd throw it away. I wouldn't buy. That's why the stenographers don't. There's nothing inviting about the way you package your product."

This conversation took place just at the time many of my friend's competitors had learned to wrap their goods in transparent coverings so that the purchaser might see what he was getting. I told him to follow their example, placing a simple white band on the outside like a bright napkin ring. In less than a month the company was out of the red.

A simple little suggestion, you tell me, since it had already been adopted by competing firms. Yet people, and corporations, still fail because they do not follow the underlying principle.

The only way to interest anyone in anything is by a

wise approach to his selfishness. This is quite as true when dealing with a full-fledged sacrificial idealist as with a Shylock. Even a consecrated charity worker is concerned with what you say in relation to his task. He wants to be successful in his ministry.

Intelligence is the satisfier of appetite. We use our wits to fulfill our longings. Ignore this and you won't sell your candy—or your ideas. Accept it, and you gain the co-operation of your children, yes, even of your wife.

If, after all, self-preservation is a major drive with you, isn't this true of anyone with whom you must deal? Consider his interest and needs. Study how to bring him more comfort and fuller power. You need not then struggle for his response.

When a small boy wants his playmate to come over to his house, he goes over to the friend's place to get him. This is an act of wisdom. When you want a man to think your way, go into his mind and find something he's thinking that you can join him in. Then invite him to come over into your mulling for a while.

But don't expect him to like it if your wits are in a mess. Intellectual comradeship requires that you think your thoughts through to the place where you can make the complex seem simple, the obscure quite clear. No one knows what he is talking about until he can put it in such lucid language that his wife's relatives understand him.

One of our scientific men used to have a teddy bear on his desk. He tried to make his technical facts so plain that even the teddy could give his approval. That is an art.

Some years ago, I boarded a train for a small eastern city. The journey took five hours. In the club car was a foreign-looking man. We began to talk. I found he was a cook; a chef in one of the great New York hotels. We had a grand time. He told me many interesting facts about the psychology of food, the strange eating preferences of people. On my return journey, I found another man in the Pullman. He was president of a cattle breeders' association. We began to talk. We had a grand time. He told me all about the biology of cattle breeding, information that connected directly with the character traits of humanity. The art of conversation is simple. Find what interests you in the other person's thought.

Successful talk follows the rule of good journalism: start with what is familiar to your listener and move gradually to the unfamiliar. Do not fling your major facts into your companion's face. Bluntness is the sign of a dull pencil and a duller intellect. Stop to prepare your presentation so that a series of graded values, from what your companion believes up to what you wish to convince him about, makes a stairway for him to reach your conclusion.

Most conversations are ruined before they begin. Too many people have the idea that a successful discussion is developed by objecting to what your companion is saying before you understand what he is talking about.

Learn to say: "Do you mean?" "Was this your idea?" "Let me restate your thought in my own terms, I'm not so good at getting it otherwise." Be willing even to word what others are feeling to find what their fears imply. But don't shame them by your skill in voicing their intentions. There is nothing more unpleasant than one who can flow like an open spigot with what he's sure is everyone else's inarticulate broodings. "I know you meant this, my dear, but didn't dare to say it," should be a justified cause for homicide. Since you care so much for your own rights, it isn't foolish to suppose others care also.

Advocates of high-power methods prate of arousing enthusiasm in others, as if it were in listening that excitement starts. The idea is mistaken. A dead brain brings no one else to life. You arouse enthusiasm in others by your own ardor. That which fires you may set someone else aflame. We should be busy living life so vitally that response in others is assured. Never tinker with anyone's passion. Let his feelings alone. Release yours and if they burn brightly his warmth will follow.

When my father wished to persuade anyone of something, he used to tell them how he was persuaded. He brought no pressure to bear, but explained why his point meant so much to him. And—as I recall it—he was invincible, even with his family.

Many writers of sales courses talk about the art of holding another person's attention. Such an idea is bunkum. You can't *hold* anyone's attention. You must find where it is, and when you bring your interests into his focus you have what you want him to consider in his line of vision. You want money. If I can prove to you that some of the obligations you thought were necessary expenses can be honorably dropped off, and your conscience still be clear, I don't have to use high-powered salesmanship to gain your attention.

The best way of getting people to do what you desire is to remove so utterly the pressure most people put upon them that your amiable vacuum acts like a suction pump. No one wants to be kind because you make him feel he should be. He wishes to surprise you with his generosity when you make it clear he needn't lift his finger on your behalf.

In any case, never force anyone to compromise his right of choice, nor expect to hold his attention by casual appeals to his egotism. The will of his stomach is far more impelling than the pull of his pride.

25   *Business Faces a Crisis*

The scene is typical of the private office of almost any manufacturing company. Time: November, an election year.
Characters:
John Standish, president of the Standish Tool Co.
Jack Standish, his son, vice-president.
Max Ford, the company's treasurer.
Curt Holden, employment manager and shop superintendent.
Bert Bitterman, a detective.

John Standish stands in his office window. The Empire State Building towers above him. The lights are beginning to glow, but nothing twinkles in the manufacturer's mind. The problem of his business shuts out the view and transforms the silver twilight into a cloudy night.

For weeks now his employees have been on strike. Long before the storm broke, sabotage had come to light. The company faces ruin if the situation continues. On the other hand, a rival firm is free of labor unrest and carrying on a war against Standish products.

The salesmen have been powerless to meet the methods of the competing firm, and unable to guarantee deliveries. John Standish returns to his desk, gaunt and haggard. He is waiting for a report on the situation. Newsboys in the street are heard calling the election news. With each cry Standish's face becomes more gray.

He feels sure the men, heartened by the political trend, will not be willing to yield until long after the company has gone into receivership.

A knock at the door and Ford enters, followed by Bitterman. The men are grave, though a look of pride shows in Bitterman's eyes.

"Well?" Standish looks up nervously. "What's your news, what have you found?"

"I'll let Bitterman tell you," mutters Ford wearily.

"Bitterman? Why, what—" Standish sits forward.

"We've uncovered the whole situation, sir," the detective answers. "This trouble began last June. Sensing the probable trend of the labor situation, your competitor, the Smithport Utensil Company, held a directors' meeting just after the nominations were over. It was decided that business would probably be too tight for both companies to survive, so they elected to put you out of the running. They shifted to cheaper products that seem about as good, but could sell at a lower price, began granting rebates—against their understanding with you—and offered higher commissions to their salesmen for a year's period."

"I'd guessed as much already," Standish glowers.

"Did you know about the order to shop foremen in regard to hours and wages in their plant?"

"Hm—maybe, maybe—" Standish hedges, his pride hurt by any doubt of his business acumen. "You mean they are paying their men more?"

"No—that would be news that you could discover. Each Smithport foreman sees to it that no unrest develops this year at that company, and the men are playing the game because—well—they lose nothing, you know, if you are broken first. I think some of them suspected what was to happen here."

"What was to happen? What do you mean?"

"I mean Schwarz, Olmsby, Bambosa and the strike

committee are Smithport men, still in their employ. They were sent here to organize a strike, in order to put you out. The scheme is one of business competition."

"My God, can you prove that?" Standish is purple in the face.

"Yes, sir. We've all the facts."

"You mean they are using labor unrest to their own ends?"

"They think they are." Bitterman's laugh holds a sneer. "It'll be their turn next, but after the receivers are through with you."

Jack Standish and Curt Holden enter. A flash almost of resentment comes over the senior Standish's face as he turns to greet his son.

"You've heard the news?"

"Yes, Dad, some hours ago. You remember what I told you."

"I never could have believed it," mutters Standish brokenly, "my own crowd."

"Your own enemies, Father—both in fact and in philosophy."

"I don't want any of your theories."

"I know you don't, but you've got to take them—now."

"I'll take nothing of the sort."

"Then you'd better give up before this situation kills you. There's only one way to win."

"What way?" Ford demands. Fear and anger brood in the eyes of the company's little treasurer, but he speaks like a man who dimly sees a warning he has hitherto refused to face.

"The way of intelligent selfishness," the young man snaps out vigorously. "Just before he died, Otto Kahn remarked that he'd rather save a tenth of his fortune than none of it. He explained to me his idea of intelligent selfishness. It consisted in seeing what was happening in the world in which one lived and in suiting one's ways of self-preservation to the situations with which one must deal. He reminded me that we haven't refused to change our manufacturing methods as times have changed, but many have refused to change employment methods. That's why we're in this pickle."

Jack's father rises: "I'll have you mind your—"

"Wait a minute," Max Ford interrupts. "It'll do no good now to damn your boy. We mustn't quarrel among ourselves. What do you think caused this strike, Jack?"

"Ask Holden. He manages the men."

"How about it, Curt?"

"Because they have a grievance," the superintendent answers.

"You say that?" Standish shouts. "You're a traitor to—"

"Come, come, John." Ford pushes his superior back into his seat. "Holden is heart and soul with us, and you know it. You don't think they'll yield, Curt?"

"Never in the world."

"Then we're done for," Ford groans.

"We're not done for, if I can get you and Father to use some common sense and begin to think in the ways of this century instead of those of your grandfathers." Young Standish is on his feet now. "You've got two facts to face: the dishonest trickery of the Smithport crowd, and the organized unrest of the men. Fight both and you lose. You can only beat your enemy by winning the cooperation of your employees. You've played with the Bourbons and they sold you out. You need someone's loyalty."

The detective has sat watchfully through all the discussion, but as he listens to the firm's junior member, the subtle sneer leaves his face. He is paying deep attention. Ford catches the responsiveness of his expression.

"You believe this, Bitterman?" he demands.

"Nothing was ever more right, or more inevitable. You can't conquer between two enemies."

"I've told you this for some time," Holden adds quietly.

"What would you do then?" Ford presses.

"Reorganize on more than modern lines," Jack Standish cries. "Reorganize as several other companies have done. Take the men in. Give them a voice in the affairs of the firm. Introduce cooperative methods. Beat the Smithport people by honestly doing with our mechanics what they pretend to do. Their turn will come, and we'll be as strong as we advertise our products to be. Get half of the efficiency into our labor methods we have in our manufacturing processes and nothing can touch us."

One might go on with the dramatic story of how the Standish Tool Company met its challenge and readjusted itself to the demands of the hour, but the principles of its final decision are more important to us here than the details of its reconstruction. The point of view that Jack Standish was endeavoring to make his father see wasn't necessarily a liberal labor attitude, or an example of the more radical thought of the younger generation in relation to economic and social problems. It is a principle of life. It relates to any and every crisis.

"Intelligent selfishness," Otto Kahn had called it, and I know just what the wise banker meant, for he disclosed his ideas to me not many weeks before he left such matters far behind him. One couldn't have called Kahn a revolutionary, or a communist. He was frankly interested in maintaining all he could of the capitalist power, which goes so inherently with the banking life to which he was accustomed.

It was merely that Kahn was a practical thinker, who understood what adjustment means. He knew that there are times when it pays to win by losing, or putting it another way: if you don't lose first, you won't win afterward. Such a constructive nonresistance is the truest strategy in the face of such a crisis as the Standish Company was dealing with.

After all, Jack was only pleading for a practical application of the basic law of personality. The men in the company were fighting against compromise of themselves and of their working conditions. We can battle for years on this issue. It will never cease until we learn that free men will be free, will struggle endlessly against compromise of their sense of selfhood. Nor shall we get anywhere in handling such dilemmas until we learn to give up ego satisfactions and put our attention on mutual welfare and intelligent cooperative action.

Reduced to simplicity, here is the spirit of Jack's solution:

Six Points for Trouble Solving

1. Fair play is not a matter of morals but of intelligence.
2. To be a good loser is sometimes essential to winning. Not otherwise is the world on your side.
3. The group never accepts a competitive spirit, except for the sake of the group.
4. If you share your self-interest with others, you can keep it yourself.
5. You get freedom of action by granting it to all with whom you deal.
6. When in doubt, ask some opponent what he thinks is the honest thing to do.

26   *Love Isn't Enough*

All his life Bert Fredrickson had been in difficulties: first one kind, then another. He didn't seem to deserve it either. He wasn't greedy or unkind; he didn't meet people with a grouch when they came in. Nor was he especially neurotic, causing upsets by emotional sensitivity. Yet trouble tagged him. All the philosophies about doing "good to others and they will do good to you" failed in his case.

They fail in any case when life is met as Bert handled it. And that's the sad fact. There are two sides to this problem of living: the love side, and the wisdom aspect. You can be gracious, generous, kindly, courteous, cooperative, conscientious and courageous, and fail—fail utterly—if you aren't skillful.

Love alone isn't enough. It needs its mate: wisdom. Ignorance takes its toll first, last and always. Affection cannot win without understanding.

It is tragic that so many good-hearted people go through life believing that love is all-powerful. It is unfortunate that no one tells them soon enough that the world trades on goodness, enslaves it, imprisons it, without an alert sagacity to protect and guide it. Power is the son of wisdom, born out of love.

"Why didn't someone tell me this before?" Mr. Fredrickson cried, as we sat together one afternoon and I explained the causes of his failures.

"Because the world is still sentimental where human conduct is concerned. It doesn't reduce life to actuals in the moral realm. It depends on the suppositions of antiquity. When we merely try to do good with loving kindness for all, we dim our wits and cannot, therefore, avoid a compromise of ourselves. To apply the magic formula, or to obey the laws of selfhood, one must think. Judgment is needed. It fails us if we pull a veil of sentimentality over our eyes.

"Let us study for a few minutes just how foolish your thinking has been, because you expected love instead of wisdom to solve your riddles. A close survey of your conduct in the trouble you've had shows the following mistakes:

"You've allowed distractions to divert your attention because you were afraid of what people would say; afraid they would think you selfish.

"You've taken on the feelings and moods of others, merging with the turmoil of their troubles: an evil form of unselfish sympathy.

"You've put your moral prejudices and biases in the way of situations until you could no longer see them clearly, and all from a fear of being yourself.

"Because of guilt decisions, you've let scores of past failures color your present trouble and viewed present quandaries in an infantile way, as punishment for your sins.

"You've become emotionally worked up over a trouble until you couldn't think, secretly believing yourself to be selfish, and punishing yourself so much that you've distorted your reason.

"You've had rigid ways of judging things, moral precepts; and you let these dogmas become the surrogates for judgment, forcing you to attach abnormal emotional meanings to plain facts.

"You've made a pretense of adaptation that was

overacted, from a feeling that you ought to be perfect, then turned cynical and skeptical when your idealism failed. Self-doubt followed. That is why you tried to prove yourself invariably right. Then you failed to keep any perspective or detachment, becoming self-conscious and imprisoned in nervousness.

"If you'd believed that wisdom was essential to love, and self-development as important as any unselfishness, you would have kept your head and used your wits in an orderly manner. When you found yourself confronted by a difficulty, you would have arranged the facts and forms of that problem until you could visualize them. Then, tracing all the relations you could observe, correlating inner and outer facts, causes and effects, you would have tried to see the subjective values, trends, tendencies and cues, connecting the abstract with the concrete.

"Finally you would have assembled and linked all previously gathered material from your memory, letting each new fact relate to your past experiences. Thus, you would have made these memory images powerful tools by reducing the main facts to ideas, and attempted to find a motive in each of them; what we call a 'constant among the variables.'"

Now, you may call this a scientific way of describing orderly and intelligent thought, but it is also simple if you are willing to see it. I was, of course, only asking Mr. Fredrickson to use the type of thinking in his personal problem that he required of himself as a chemist. He is living in an actual world where his circumstances are as much affected by laws and principles as are those in a laboratory. If you mix the wrong chemicals, you'll get an explosion, or a poison. If you mix the wrong people, you get an uproar or a mess.

Nature brooks no disobedience of her laws. She hurts us just as much when we are loving and ignorant as when we are hateful and stupid. We suffer from mistakes in any case. Not once has any man been excused by her for good motives. Thoughtless obedience to man-made creeds does nothing to save us. Surrender is the only solution: surrender to the laws of life.

27   *How Trouble Grows*

Troubles come upon us gradually. When Clarence Watson yielded to his wife's request and took her brother, Frank, into his business, it looked like a simple act of kindness. Nor had he thought it a fatal step when they arranged for Grace's mother to live with them. It was, after all, a natural thing. Few would deny that a mother would like to have her son with her most of the time, thought Clarence, when his brother-in-law came to be there also.

Situations have a way of growing up about you, or on you, before you know it, and in a million indirect ways. There was no perceptible line of change between the first yielding to Grace's wishes and the ultimate burden on Clarence, in a situation that left him no rest and required him to let a fretful woman ruin his marriage.

There was no place where the pressure became endurable. Nor had Grace herself made any marked change in her attitude. Her love for Clarence had merely ebbed with each new responsibility he assumed;

ebbed because the more he did for her relatives, the less he could do for her.

Have you ever noticed this mysterious contradiction: that those who toil unmercifully for others lose the love of those for whom they sacrifice? It is not only a fact but the fulfillment of a law. People love us for what we are. As we disappear under the burdens they put on us, they unconsciously blame us for the loss of our charm which the burdens create.

Few of us are worried, however, while situations are growing. We do not at the time recognize them as serious. It is when we find ourselves submerged that the crises come. To get out of them would mean a repudiation of the philosophy that let us get into them.

What could Clarence do to free himself in his situation without gaining the hatred of his mother-in-law, the ill will of his brother-in-law and wage a bitter, punitive battle with his wife? And if his "conscience" were still vulnerable, still as sick and fear-ridden as that of most men, would he not, had he tried to correct his crushing problem, have carried such guilt that remorse might well have killed him?

Is there any answer to such a situation and to millions of unjust and evil conditions identical with Clarence's except a repudiation of the degenerate practices that permitted them to be? And must we not, when imprisoned in such agonizing dilemmas, cast from our souls any belief in these superstitions, becoming thereby immune to the sentimental mouthings of those who are minders of other people's business?

Freedom comes only from seeing the ignorance of your critics and discovering the emptiness of their virtue.

Troubles grow about us only because we let them, only when we don't apply the tenets of integrity. He who will not compromise himself at any time soon sees when situations are creeping up on his primary relation to life. Nor is his refusal one of petulant pride or ego satisfaction. He dares to resist, dares to turn a trouble topsy-turvy, having faith that in the end his act is best for all. A compromise of yourself leads inevitably to compromise of others.

You and I are caught between two evils. Moralists on the one hand teach a destructive and impractical ethic, a doctrine of self-denial that no man could apply and not become a titmouse. Men follow a procedure as opposite to this supine unselfishness as the lunge of a panther differs from the quiver of a jellyfish.

We have been left for centuries with only the echo of a workable philosophy. We have been given no true middle way between insipid spirituality and brute conquest: either act like a stained-glass saint or ape a tyrant.

The situation is even worse than this, for our wits have been cut in two by this despoiling of intelligence. More than half of our power lies submerged. Freud and his followers have written much about the unconscious mind. Rather should we see it as suppressed, driven back and filled full of guilt by the pressure of our conventions and the ignorance of our shibboleths.

We are in a situation in which thousands go insane because their intellects move forward while their emotions pull back. They do not know the data of corruption directly traceable to this Golden Calf the Pharisees have erected.

Nor do they understand that seldom is there virtue in the masochistic martyrdom people miscall goodness. Most of the pressure in our lives would have disappeared had we let our friends and families do their own living, the living they could do within their knowledge and capacity. We do not need to carry each other and children, mothers, brothers, upon our backs.

Life is greater than anyone's vision, deeper than all opinion. To penetrate its mystery is essential. Insight requires a conjunction with reality. It is this contact with the actual which life asks of us. Its purpose is not to make us carry sorrows, or even to endure our own. Experience serves to quicken our alertness so that good, not bad, may come to pass.

All this being the case, there are seven important rules in handling trouble:

1. Don't attempt anything you may not be able to finish.
2. Don't measure a situation by what it is, but by what it can become.
3. Remember that trouble grows silently, stealthily, unbelievably and continually.
4. Have the wisdom to see it may become unendurable in your case.
5. Have the courage to reject trouble before it starts.
6. Don't believe it when your intimates tell you: "It couldn't become serious." It could, and usually does.
7. When you are in a situation that has grown up about you, have the nerve to get out of it—*now*. It will continue to grow worse and become unbearable if you let it.

Everything and everybody has a saturation point. This means you. The time will come when you can stand no more from the people and things who fill you with fury. Whoever and whatever they are: wives, sisters, mothers, fathers, husbands, partners, bosses, hours, neighborhoods, jobs, jostling crowds or jazzy visitors, it makes no difference if the irritation they create grows faster than you can give it outlet, you will someday slop over and make a mighty splash. If such a saturation is inevitable, is it not better to change now, move in, move out, give up, invite some relative to leave, or leave yourself before the explosion?

Unless you make the "psychological moment," it unmakes you. Failure springs from dilatory thinking. Half the art of living lies in alertness. Life is full of opportunities, a stream of little chances. Few hours are great, few seconds momentous, unless we have gathered the minor occasions into a salient. He who marshals his psychological moments as a general lays his strategy never has to await their advent.

If you haven't dared, because of your ethical strictures, to deal sturdily with your difficulties, you doubtless have the habit of getting people to justify your mistakes. If you didn't dare marry the woman you loved because to do so meant leaving mother, it's easy to find a million disappointed pessimists to tell you how noble was your sacrifice.

You always sin when you deny yourself for a purpose below your possibilities. Suppose Jesus had denied his power to teach and heal to satisfy a desire of his family to have him build them a new house! Unselfishness of this sort is evil, an evil advocated and praised by millions.

You sin when you endure such a situation as grew up around Clarence Watson, but not when you have the integrity to get out of it. The worst thing about self-sacrifice as commonly practiced is its dishonesty. There is a stench about it, a reeking psychic odor of decaying egotism.

Self-neglect is a form of suicide, a first step in the destruction of one's nature. This psychic self-destruction usually precedes the actual taking of one's life. Somewhere the evil doctrine of patient endurance has been at work. The final killing of one's body is but a completion of the sacrifice.

28   *How to Handle Gossip*

Gossip is the instrument of virtue, as virtue is commonly regarded. Gossip is the weapon of moral cruelty, a remnant of the days when people were tortured at the stake. There is no word so powerful, if you fear it, and none so impotent if you know it is a sham.

There is, however, no way to advise anyone to handle gossip unless he has chosen obedience to nature and the guidance of science as his way of life.

A score of troubles may front you, from believing in social doctrines antagonistic to your set, to loving a married woman. You belong to the Union League, yet would plead the rights of labor. You are a D.A.R. yet work for peace. You live among fundamentalists, your father is one of them, you are not. As long as the lashes of your critics mean more to you than noise, there is no solution. Every experience through which you pass is a test of what you believe.

Freedom on the inside is the only freedom. Indifference to the world, no matter what its attitude, is the only protection. The first principle in handling any and every trouble is independence, not only as to the consequences of your decision but from the verdict of society. Without this, any and all advice, except the most slavish acceptance of the will of the group, is useless.

The third step in the removal of irritation lies in a cleavage to the doctrine of personal integrity. If you follow what you believe, if you do the best you can from the basis of your standard of truth, no man has a right to fault you. There is no other honesty, no other happiness.

Matilda Harroway lives in a neighborhood that talks and talks. It seldom bothers itself about her. What's the use? It doesn't make Matilda suffer, and no one gossips when it produces no results. In fact, it is something of an affront to build up a story about a businesswoman who lives as Matilda does and not have her mind it in the least.

If you would be free from the curse of gossip, you must also come to your own verdict as to the gossipmongers. If you see them as the vultures of a dying age, who feed on the carrion of censoriousness, you smile as you would at any buzzard on an old dead tree. You will have sympathy, too, for your less sturdy fellows who live in terror of breaking the ancient codes. You will see them adjusting so painfully to the minor social requirements that they never achieve a primary purpose. Secondary adaptation becomes their creed. The right clothes must be worn to church. Belief in the religion taught there is not important: a bridal veil of the proper length at all costs; the question of loving the man you marry is incidental.

They tend to focus on phantasies instead of facts, accepting the masquerade of civilization and miscalling it life. They decide on mimic values when the camouflage of culture becomes a standard of credit. They are futile in decision, substituting sophistications for intelligent judgment.

You will see, too, that judgers of others have crafty consciences. You will find that reformers are the ones who need help. That is why they took to making the world over. When evils press within a man, it is easier to deal with faults in others. For that reason, he who blames you deserves it. His condemnation is admission of evil in himself. When an Arabian harlot reformed for one night, she begged the police to arrest all harlots. The more vicious such a woman's heart, the more readily she condemns her companions.

Virulence is manufactured from our memories. The man who deflowered virgins as a boy fears his daughter will be the victim of rape. He who was an onanist in his youth dreads masturbation in his son. Blaming is an index of ancient guilt. Such a person knows your duty and quickly tells you of it. Decent people are silent before the awful responsibility of seeing the true.

The pet device of gossipmongers is to call any and all solutions you offer for the correction of your woe "dangerous, extreme and immoral." For Juliet to love Romeo was dangerous. For the former king, Edward, to care for the welfare of the poor was "extreme." For him to have loved Mrs. Simpson was "immoral." Thus do all cowards and despoilers fear honest affection and forthright courage.

Little souls wish you to be unhappy. It aggravates them to have you joyous, efficient and free. They like to feel that fate is disciplining you. It gives their egos wings if yours are clipped. You can ruin your life in an hour by listening to their puerile opinions.

Did you ever notice how hypocrites love the trappings of virtue? They know all the sentimental gunk, all the claptrap of goodness. I have never seen a sneak thief who didn't worship the moral code, both in and out of church.

The camouflage of self-sacrifice, so apparent in censorious people, should be enough to warn decent citizens. You are known by the company you keep, and if you run with these prowlers of pornography they will know you are as full of lust.

As long as you accept such moral teaching with the

same credulity the followers of the Inquisition showed for their perverted doctrine, you will also accept the other social abnormalities that are filling our asylums. With such delusions in your head, you cannot solve your problems. Nor can you escape gossip.

The responsibility for accepting the morals of your land and time has been held before people always. The herd-minded believe it unthinkingly, or rationalize their compromise as "necessary." Honest folk cannot yield to external values without rebellion. A South Sea island girl, whose father attempts to sell her into prostitution, might, if she were herd-minded, yet cared for love in its reality, become devasted in consequence. Those who advocate the moral standards of the group as they happen to be would counsel the girl to let herself be despoiled and to give up her ideals as the way to avoid trouble.

We, who see maladjustment as a fault of society rather than of personality, would counsel her to revolt against the demands of her community, yet at the same time we would teach her to forgive her father as one who is ignorantly following the ways of his tribe. She might sorrow at having to flee her home and go against the responsibility of her setting, but she would not have a breakdown because of her decision.

Conquerors practice fulfillment of self. Abnegators allow situations to become their masters. We cope with tasks efficiently if attention toward them is unhampered by doubt. We fail when superstitions interfere. It isn't luck but relief that rules your life.

The question of ability is important if by it we mean the intelligence to see foolishness and ignore taboos. The wits that win are those that function without dread, dread of the consequences of being oneself. A mighty lesson was given by Polonius to Laertes: "To thine own

self be true, and it must follow as the night the day,
thou canst not then be false to any man."

No situation at any time requires compromise. You
only think it does. Dare to despise distortions of your
nature, constrictions of normal growth, and you will
solve your problems.

29 A Marriage Dilemma

It was one of those brisk autumn days that Kate so
loved. On this particular afternoon, golden leaves might
have fallen all around her without so much as gaining
a glance. She walked rapidly, thinking fast. She might
as well talk to Barbara, she just had to tell somebody.
Peter was so obtuse. He never saw below the surface of
anything. Tears were only tears to him.

The crisis in her marriage came upon Kate suddenly.
She had long ago adjusted herself to her husband's immaturity. She was used to his absorbed inattention and
sexual ineptitude. The little romantic touches had
ceased with their honeymoon. She could handle his
neglect of Helen and Marie. A father couldn't be expected to understand two strange, sensitive girls.

It was the loneliness that got her. She recalled her
girlhood, filled with music and brilliant conversation.
There had been drama and beauty in life then, good
plays to see, books to discuss. Peter, calling it "high-
brow," turned jazz on the radio when she wanted to talk.

The gaiety of Barbara's house had a healing effect.

She hated to spoil a lovely afternoon with her tale of woe, yet before she knew it the drab story came tumbling out.

"I can't stand it any longer," she ended.

Barbara had listened with now and then a sympathetic word. Then she spoke.

"Of course this isn't news to me, Kate dear. Jim and I have discussed it, though we've never spoken of it to anyone. People mostly know, or somehow feel, what the marriage of a friend is like. Sometimes they know the cause. I'm sure that all you say is true. Peter is immature, and only concerned with surface interests. His business absorbs him. When he's home, he wants to be amused."

"But he chooses such silly ways of doing it," Kate broke in. "I never get half of his attention. He complains about expenses, but won't arrange a budget. When I bring up difficulties, he thinks I'm complaining."

"And after a fuss, he stays away for a night or so, I suppose," Barbara queried.

Kate nodded dumbly. "I—I used to think there was another woman, but I guess it isn't so."

"But there is, my dear. There's always another woman," Barbara answered slowly.

Then, seeing the anguish in her friend's eyes, she added: "In this case, it's not one of flesh and blood. You had your dream of the man you hoped to marry. He was to understand you—really. Peter has his dream wife too. He married one quite different from his phantasy of a perfect mate. And now he's not trying to save his marriage. He's going through the motions of a dull husband."

"But Babs, he always expects me to think and feel just as he does. He never considers my longings."

"Does he have to, Kate?"

"Shouldn't he? Can one have much of a marriage any other way?"

"No, you can't. What I meant was that you seem to have been trying to hold your home together by giving up all interests that conflict with those of your husband. You've tried to shape yourself to his ways. You've sacrificed your music, your fondness for good plays, your literary friends."

"But shouldn't I? It seems selfish not to, since they bore Peter."

"But look at the result. You've become dull too, and the worst of it is, you're dull to Peter. He used to adore you and sometimes put himself out for you. He thought you charming. Now, he's indifferent. He hasn't turned to another woman yet—only in his fancy. But he will, for you are dying on your feet. Self-effacement such as you practice will never solve a marriage. It ruins it."

"You mean I should do the things I love to do?"

"Didn't you while you were engaged to Peter?"

"Why, of course."

"And didn't he love you then?"

"He worshiped me."

"Well, there's your answer. Stop trying to fit yourself into the little mold you think is his wife pattern. Become the vivacious, life-loving Kate you used to be. Then see what happens. Peter isn't as hopeless or as dull as you think. He's quite interesting when he has to be."

Kate looked up suddenly, searching her friend's face. "Has he talked to you, Babs?" she demanded.

"Every man talks to any woman who will listen. You try being the old Kate and see what he does."

About a month later, Peter Barnes stepped off his commuting train with a boyish swing. He couldn't have told you why, but life had become more interesting of late. As he had objected violently to Kate's recent activities, they couldn't have brought the new note. But

Kate herself, now. She was somehow different, or was
it different? She seemed like her old self again, the girl
he'd adored in their college days. There was color in
her cheeks that wasn't all put on, and a sparkle in her
eyes as if she had a wonderful secret. Most of all, her
humor had come back—the daredevil wit that used
to sally forth like a comical parrot. Something had happened.

A few weeks later Kate went to see Barbara again.

"My dear," she cried, "if you learned your marital
wisdom from having been a social worker, I recommend
it for all wives. It may be psychology, as you say, but
to me it's uncommon sense. I know now what you mean
when you tell me that one's own happiness is the secret
of success in intimacy. You can't give joy to your partner unless you have it to give, and you can't have it if
you are starved by a silly compromise. No, my dear,
I'm through with being a dutiful slavey in the home, working and waiting like a sick scullery maid for my master's return. Sometimes I'm there, sometimes I'm not,
but when I am there, it's a live woman not a dead wife
he finds. I'm not a pig about it either, I do a lot more of
the things he likes because I'm getting my own satisfactions."

Only when we refuse all compromises of the self in
marriage, yet wisely refrain from coercing the mate, is
the relationship ever a success. Adapt we must, through
a tender understanding of failings in which we share,
but this does not mean, nor necessitate, perversions of
the personality. Marriage requires more cooperation
than any other relation, a dynamic fulfillment of mutual
aid. Its happiness permits no thoughtless neglect, no ego
satisfactions. *You cannot do and say anything you choose*.
You cannot retire into yourself, or coddle your peeves.
What you do must be for the welfare of both.

There is a principle in this situation that Kate did

not know about. We are constituted with a rhythm in our makeup, a rhythm as definite as day and night. Failure to recognize it causes anguish for millions. You cannot keep a constant focus on a loved one, no matter how much you love her. You cannot focus exclusively on achievement, no matter how your work enthralls you. You swing between the erotic and the dynamic aspects of consciousness.

This alternation is biological and organic. It is also psychical. It functions in the nature of woman quite as definitely as in man. The old idea "man's love is of man's life a thing apart; 'tis woman's whole existence," is piffle. Woman's love is quite as separated from her life when she is pursuing her dynamic interests as that of any man. Our forefathers put women in a jail of domesticity and procreation. They wished her whole existence to be for them. Under this curse, women sickened and died. The social restriction kept them conveniently on tap, but what anemic and frigid creatures they became!

He who prefers the responsiveness of a modern woman must accept the fact that her rhythm is as marked as his own, nor will she always be amative just when he is, or absorbed in her work when he is busy. She fails in perpetual devotion just as he does. There are times of intimacy, others of passivity.

A little study and some skill in seeking for compatibility in this vibration will do much to harmonize it. You can, if you will, find the tempo of your mate and teach yourself adaptation to his or her swing.

If both partners have this purpose, a balance between the rhythms is established, a harmony of romantic absorption and dynamic expansion that vitalizes love and achievement. In marriage the art of selfishness reaches its highest expression. They who keep their charm and their interests bring joy to the mate.

Eugene has worked his way into advertising after several years' experience as a reporter, and a period as a traveling salesman. His is a convivial nature, but not unduly so. After his marriage, Henrietta's Aunt Priscilla came to live with them. She is a woman with strong ideas but a sensitive nature. For her sake they moved into an expensive suburb. Did you ever see a hairless dog in a patch of stinging nettles? Eugene liked Maple Manor quite as cordially.

Their style of life denied him the vacations he used to have in the Canadian woods. He had stood the city then, with the thought of those weeks in the heart of nature. Now he couldn't afford them. His dream of someday having a ranch and living an outdoor life glimmered more and more faintly. It looked as if his sentence to hard labor was for life.

No one, not even his wife, ever gave his need a thought. Wasn't he the good provider? Henrietta and Priscilla were content. They had their club life, their afternoons for bridge, their summers out in the graden, solaces typical of America. You gather that this was an average setting.

The scene of our story opens in a lawyer's office. Henrietta has gone to John Craige to have him arrange a separation. She cannot go on. She wishes to have Eugene let her keep the Maple Manor home, or else take the children and go to Florida. If he'll give her half his income, and an allowance for Aunt Priscilla, she can get along. The situation, you see, is typical. No one could expect a highly bred, sensitive woman, like Henrietta, to put up with intoxication. No, no, of course not.

At this point, the narrative develops a surprise twist. John Craige doesn't see things through Henrietta's eyes. He questions Henrietta and discovers that under her maudlin Maple Manorishness, and Aunt Priscilla-itis, is a real woman. Secretly she still loves Eugene.

John decides to save the marriage if he can. To do so, he must make Henrietta face what their life is to Eugene. He must get Priscilla out of the home to which she clings like a sick snail. But that is not all. Being a man of experience, he senses the true center of the situation: that Henrietta has become frigid, the victim of what is called "aprasexia"; an inability to pay attention to any aspect of intimacy; a condition common to women distracted by callers, clubs, children, neighbors, shopping and a thousand other things considered "necessary."

Craige makes Henrietta see that Eugene's drinking is not only an escape from boredom, but a solace for the collapse of his sex life. He asks her what consideration she has had for the fearful strain Eugene lives under in his office, and whether she knows how she used him as a provider for her maternal glory.

He shows her that no man, who has spent years working his way to success, is normal in his amative capacity, and that often he's too tired and confused to take any initiative. Eugene had to inhibit himself for years, he explained, and needs to be released from his self-repression by outgoing love and erotic stimulation. Unless she is willing to take as much initiative as alcohol takes, helping Eugene to relax and to find lift and ecstasy when with her, the attempt will fail. If it fails, she must be willing to admit that she, by the life she demands for herself and her family, causes his condition.

We need not go into the discussion that followed. Henrietta, if she remained with Eugene, had intended to insist that she become his guardian: managing his money, cashing the checks and limiting his spending. She expected to follow him around at cocktail parties like an anxious hen. She had, in fact, done much of this already.

To help him, instead, to find emotional outlets, to change their way of life, to move out of Maple Manor, send Aunt Priscilla away, to cut down expenses, to make a plan for their future closer to Eugene's dreams, most of all to revolutionize their sexual life and increase her responsiveness; this was no small earthquake in Henrietta's life. She did it successfully, however.

"The ecstasy of intoxication is nearest to the exhilaration of a sexual orgasm," Craige told her in his fatherly way. "See that the glory of intimacy is achieved and its sordid substitute will disappear."

There are instances, of course, when the physical body has become so involved in such a condition that one should seek medical aid. Glandular disturbances may be serious. But in general, the cure of drink begins with the correction of one's relation to life. Men drink to satiety to escape compromise, and because they have not learned that self-indulgence never pays. Ego satisfactions in the end destroy all satisfactions, taking away the response of the senses by which contentment is realized. Ignorant of this fact, men and women seek solace from:

Nagging wives or husbands	Unfair human or work
Interfering relatives	relations
Infelicity in the home	Humiliating situations
Sexual maladjustment	Intimates causing hurt feelings
An extravagant family	Arrogant associates
Parental domination	Unadjusted problems

Unmerited blame   Lack of constructive conviviality,
Hidden feelings of guilt   persistent loneliness
Serious neurosis

All of these causes may enter in some measure. One
alone is enough to create this situation. Each can be cor-
rected if the family and the individual will cooperate.
Nagging wives or husbands must be made to face their
habits. Disturbing relatives can be removed. Infelicity
can leave the home, if there's a will to banish it. "Drink
problems" disappear when the cause is cured.

31   *Sexual Maladjustment*

One of the commonest of all mistakes is for men to
believe their wives are less sexually endowed than
themselves. Marriages are ruined because of this delusion. Men speak of not wishing to be "selfish" in their
demands. Nonsense. Intimacy on the basis of accom-
modation is prostitution.

A successful sex relation is not an ego satisfaction,
but a mutual experience. Greedy lust destroys the
thrill it seeks. Freud has described this selfishness as
"masturbatus in vagina"—an apt phrase indeed. On the
other hand, any compromise of the self to perform a
"marital duty" is lewd.

Nor is it true that women are less endowed than
men. They are more so. Their natures, however, are
responsive not compulsive. They quicken to passion
when stimulated.

You often hear men speak of their "sexual problem," as if it were unsolvable. They describe woman as a "mystery," her ways as "strange." As long as they believe this bogy, little happiness will appear in the marriage bed. The French have an apt phrase: "*Il n'y a pas les femmes froides, mais les hommes maladroit.*" (There are no frigid women, only inept men.) The trouble with most unhappy husbands lies in the unhappy husbands. They are maladroit.

Of all the problems of life, this one of sexual satisfaction—considered by so many as the most difficult—is the least so if sympathy, persistence and intelligence are applied. There are many good books on this subject.* Read them if you have a sexual difficulty; not only that, study them. But don't expect success if you apply their instructions as you would directions for adjusting your carburetor. No matter-of-fact and eminently practical way into a woman's erotic consciousness is to be had. You can't approach the question as you would a better way to brush your teeth.

In fact, the main trouble with the inept husband lies in his casual and overphysical approach. Love must be wooed, wooed constantly, wooed more at sixty than at sixteen. There isn't any royal road to permanent romance, except that of actual tender, sympathetic devotion; interest, attention and artistic demonstration. Yes, I said artistic.

Art isn't necessarily self-conscious. And here again is where the books I've suggested may fail you. They will, if you apply the instruction embarrassedly. Matters will then be worse. They will, if you apply the instruction as instruction or if you apply the suggestions as applications. Don't learn them as methods. Live them as ex-

---

* *Sexual Pleasure in Marriage* by Jerome and Julia Rainer; *Sexual Adventure in Marriage,* also by the Rainers; *Sex and the Mature Man* by Dr. Louis P. Saxe and Noel B. Gerson.

pressions. Feel them. Let yourself become one with them. Let them be unconscious patterns. Don't fulfill them objectively. Yield to them subjectively, until it is as if you had always been an artist.

The best thing that could happen to any husband would be to know more of a few typical sexual dilemmas: their cause and their cure. Here are some.

Everett is seen watching his neighbor, Winnifred, out of the window. He soliloquizes as he does so about intimacy. He thinks he now loves Winnifred rather than his wife. He hardly knows the younger woman. She is a phantasy object—an escape for his suppressed sexuality.

Some days later Everett appears at Dr. Warren's office and tells him he's not feeling well; pain in the groin, upset stomach, can't sleep. He describes his wife's nervousness and irritability. She's a scene maker. The doctor listens and understands. Gradually the story comes out, even to the phantasy attachment to Winnifred.

Dr. Warren knows Winnifred, who is twenty times as sexually inhibited as Fanny. He realizes that as the emotionally sick seek the emotionally sick, so the inept choose the frigid as their dream objects. He makes Everett face the situation and shows him why he turns to a marble statue in place of his wife. More than this, he teaches him the definite steps of loving approach, the techniques of arousal so well described in books written for such needs.

Our second drama begins at 3:00 A.M. Thomas and Theodora Conrad have not been quarreling exactly, but are having one of their endless arguments that take the place of sexual union. The truth of their situation would surprise them, for neither knows that successful erotic intimacy depends upon daily kindness. Nothing so quickly produces frigidity in women, or impotence in men, as hurt feelings. The greatest destroyers of marriage happiness are faultfinding, nagging, blame and bad temper. Anger cuts an amative bond like a sword.

There is, of course, a good deal on the man's side of any marriage question. The trouble with Gerald and Hortense Wales developed because Gerald has been unable to keep his wife from "going domestic." She is absorbed in housekeeping, the children and her father's needs. Gerald feels as if he were an appendage to her domestic court. But what has he done to bring her out of it? What can he do as long as false modesty remains? Gerald is shy. His mother brought him up to feel that sex was—well—one just didn't talk about such things.

He blushes when anyone is simple, clean and frank. At heart he is a son of Eros. He would like to have a hairy chest and follow the phallus to everlasting glory.

Through the country at large there is still a hangover of the Puritan caricature. Within recent times a newspaper published the following item:

No man or woman has ever read in a Nebraska newspaper the published statement that any Nebraska woman was getting ready for a visit of the stork. In our clean Nebraska atmosphere such a publication as that would be regarded as unclean.

Their statement isn't true: Nebraska is too fine a place for that. But could we have a better example of sanctimoniousness? As the censor does much to provoke licentiousness, so is the purist the quickener of illicit relations. The libertine and the prude have a common origin.

Few, who have not had a chance to penetrate to the reality in people's hearts, know that sexually they are often quite the opposite of what they appear. Here, for example, is the inside picture of Hortense, Gerald's apparently domestic and statuesque young wife. Phantasies of an almost rapacious nature trouble her. She likes to imagine she was born in prehistoric times when there was no hindrance to sexual expression. She dreams of making her way through the primeval forest with the prowess of a lioness. Then, outdoing the voluptuous enticements of any cat, she invites the satisfaction she craves. Yet in her everyday life there is none more prim in conduct or in speech.

Suppose Gerald had understood the situation and, removing his prudery as well as hers, had made love to her, persistently, skillfully and ardently. Would not the camouflage of domesticity have disappeared? Gerald dared not be so vulgar. Was he not an intellectual? And should he not deny himself?

There is something cold and thin about the atmosphere of sacrifice. To avoid facing reality and the agony of disappointment, people withdraw from "the flesh," becoming spiritual ghosts, living at an altitude where passion is powerless. From this mountaintop, they look at trouble as one beholds a valley peasant capturing a pig.

Such a remoteness sends any woman into aprasexia, as a result of which she gains no sensation out of intimacy. Too many women, already remote from real feeling, can be rescued only by a vigorous man. Too often they love by reflection, smiling when the man smiles, giving measure for measure. This duplicating devotion may imitate passion if the masculine ardor is intense. But don't be deceived. There is no warmth in a mirror.

Put in brief form, here are a few facts that you can

pick up from the sex manuals, if you are not already educated in these matters:

A gentle but ardent approach of long duration is the most important factor in sexual success.

Masturbation in the years before marriage is rarely the cause of marital failure, but foolish guilt about it may be.

When a woman does not experience the equivalent of full satisfaction, a serious unrest affects her health.

It is not normal for a woman to be utterly passive.

The effects of intoxication are serious on sexuality. Too much alcohol destroys erotic power. Hurried relations, or those in which the crisis is too long deferred, are equally injurious.

There are methods of curing both temporary and long-standing impotence. It is your responsibility to discover them by inquiry.

There are many facts that you can discover about the more physical aspect of intimacy that can transform most unsuccessful marriages.

Unselfishness, to the point where one's personality is extinguished, destroys erotic intimacy.

Mrs. Grundy is the worst woman to consult on these matters.

Never blame or criticize an intimate for sexual incapacity, unless you wish to injure the relationship further. It is sympathy and help that is needed.

If you destroy a mate's confidence, he, or she, cannot correct the situation.

Never be proud or secretive about erotic dissatisfaction. Frankness is essential. Keep on talking until the silliness disappears.

It is a mistake to expect an intimate to understand your feelings when you haven't explained them.

And don't be condescending when you talk—that is, not to a modern man or woman.

But if you assume that sex is your right, you'll make it your wrong. Never treat a marriage partner as a possession.

Don't let a woman's tears frighten you. That's how she washes away her nervousness.

If you try to force a sexual relationship to be better than it is, you may make it worse.

Remember that no one can maintain two emotions at the same time as dominants. Sex is crowded out by rage or fear. Don't give any cause for either and love will blossom.

An intense tactile response comes only from development. The more you imagine becoming sensitive and alive, the more your nerves will cooperate.

Tumescence is made possible only by the expulsion of all extraneous thought and feeling. Don't talk about any matters of the day at such a time. Emotional concentration is the key to success.

Half of the sexual troubles trace back to the influence of parents upon the marriage partner in the premarital period. Try to get these removed by sympathetic conversation, at other times than those of sexual intimacy.

If you are ashamed of your passion, you imprison it. To feel like a prostitute and pose as a Madonna is ruinous. It is just as bad to play the saint and be the satyr.

The more sympathy you establish in everyday life, the more you'll have in the intimate relationship.

No man becomes a permanent lover until he is fully grown up. Emotional maturity is essential. The average man needs help from the average woman in this matter of developed feeling. Usually he's too resistant and conceited to be willing to seek such aid. He blames his wife for a stupidity he creates.

Every dull husband has a cold wife. The art of being inviting reaches even to the tones of your voice. Magnetism draws the coldest steel. The ancients practiced the use of musks and perfumes, and paid attention to costumes. If you don't take time to use the good odors, at least keep the bad ones away.

If you don't learn to speak with your eyes in intimacy, you'll never learn to talk successfully.

Demonstration must include a loving of the erogenous zones, else affection is futile.

A woman is ruled by periodicities. It is a man's art to know the whens as well as the hows.

There is as much art in kissing as in painting a picture. When art is lacking idiocy takes its place.

No matter how much you talk these matters over, keep some atmosphere of mystery, and beware of whom else you talk with about them. Offhand discussion of sex in a crowd is as injurious to the necessary illusive charm as promiscuity.

If you don't sustain the spirit of romance, you can't keep the potency of sex.

The purpose of sex in life is for the demonstration of conjugal affection, not for procreation. Nature uses it as a convenience, that's all.

You need to know a thousand other concrete points about manners, motions, positions and durations. That's what the medical books are for. But that information won't work unless you strive to remain a vital person. It's the only way to continue in marriage as an interesting sex object and an adequate sex partner. Submergence in the position of wife or husband destroys romance and sexual ecstasy.

Sex is a basic need. Its denial leads one to become a burden on society. Its misuse brings injury to others.

Sex is a mutual relation. Never treat it as a greedy act. Condescension in such matters is an insult.

Most important of all, remember that your behavior during the day affects your success in the close embrace. If you treat your partner like a slave, brutally, carelessly, disrespectfully, unkindly, you'll get little erotic response.

If you are more courteous to a stranger than to your intimates, you probably love yourself most, the opinions of strangers second, and maybe you don't love your partner at all.

In any case, remember that to strive for successful sexual adjustment isn't licentious. It's your privilege, no matter how inhibited your partner may be.

If your whole relation to life is through other people, it is threatened by all the weakness of human nature. If your primary relation is social, every trend of the group, each depression, all that happens to people, will overpower you. Only he who makes some basic contact with natural objects, things of the earth, its animals and trees, its minerals and mechanics—only he is safe.

He then has a strength that none can threaten. The chemist, the engineer, the botanist, the explorer, does not kill himself when trouble comes if his relation to these primaries of life is real. The greatest step in the avoidance of suicide is "back to nature," not as our sentimental fathers sent us to the land, but as modern insight sends us to reality.

Without this primary relation, every value of life is threatened. Consider the situation that led to tragedy in the life of a man we will call Frank Dural. He was a broker on the stock exchange, who took his life. The papers spoke of it as the result of business difficulties; he had bought on margin and lost his money. His yacht and his palatial home had to be sold. He was a victim, people said, of the market. But was he? If so, why did not every man who passed through financial disruption do the same thing?

The average broker will jokingly tell you his profession is well named. He is "broke" six or eight times in his career. He seldom becomes desperate, for he expects to "come back." Investigation has revealed that only in a small percentage of the instances in which people have taken their own lives was financial worry responsible. Personal maladjustment was the cause.

Even as a boy, Dural was nervous and excitable. His mother so pampered him that he had excessive confidence in his own judgment. That he had a keen mind, none could deny. But a clever brain is one thing, careful thought another. Dural used his mind with zest, thinking at high speed and deciding on impulse. All through his twenty-two years of business experience, he lived in a state of frenzy: buying, selling, spending, entertaining madly.

For him there was no reality except the money god. The beauties of nature, the mysteries of art, the majesties of music, all were neglected. He had no time to read. The needs of his wife he met by paying bills. He would have been the first to hoot the idea that he was sick, for he thought of illness in terms of stomachaches and bad colds.

As long as the market mounted, he succeeded. When failure came, only the shreds of life were left. Nothing meant anything any more. He felt an enormous futility and a bitter cynicism. It wasn't worth the effort to get back his wealth and position, and without them there was nothing. What would have made life vivid to a normal person had been left out of his experience. Do you wonder that he gave up the struggle?

Was he tired of life, however, or society? Were the sky and the sun and the rain so bad? Was the adventure of doing what he could with the drama of events so unpleasant, except that he believed he must live in certain ways and accept circumstantial and social limitations which destiny seemed to put upon him?

If he could have lightened the business obligations

and marital requirements, social fetishes and foolish creeds, been free from the rulership of those false gods, would he have found it so hard? What was he discouraged about? Had he dared to venture into life itself, discarding with glee the mad precepts and stupid mannerisms with which he had hitherto been identified, would he have wished to destroy himself?

Bottled up in a destructive setting, bound by duty madness to a false responsibility, the soul rages at its imprisonment. Suicide is melancholia in an extreme, and as depression is built on rage that life is not more satisfactory, so we find in suicide a mechanism of revenge. The individual wishes to punish the world and those in it with whom he has come into intimate contact, because they seem to make him unhappy.

Suicide, then, is an act of ego satisfaction. Self-killers are venting their displeasure in exactly the spirit of a child in a tantrum, destroying themselves from the mad belief they must otherwise compromise, taking their lives instead of their liberties.

Such an emotional turmoil creates physical sickness and disease, toxic conditions of the blood and torpid states of the organism. Dysfunction of the endocrine system, the pituitary gland in particular, is noticeable. It is probable that wise therapy would make a remarkable "rescue" in such cases.

Habits of nervous tension are also evident in morbid conditions. Suicide follows periods of strain. We may think of it as momentary insanity, tension reaching such a pitch that coagulation develops for a time in the brain. If the agonizer knew how to relax and wait a while, the impulse would pass.

Neurotic emotionalism is the most important aspect in all courting of death. Frustration of the life wish and turbid erotic dissatisfaction are contributing factors. They lie behind the surface explanations of economic collapse and the disappointments of objective experience usually blamed for the tragic termination.

He who contemplates suicide should consider how he is being deluded by:

The presence of curable hidden disease.
A glandular imbalance, causing upsets and depressions.
Nervous tension that will pass.
A neurotic condition that is correctable.
An economic situation that will change.
Intellectual confusion from moral delusions.
Spiritual suppression from materialism.

There is no escape from the law of the Cosmos. You have your victory to win sometime, somewhere. Better win it right now.

Depressed people need a psychic high enema to help get rid of some:

Secret revenge motives.
Deluding duty patterns.
Hidden weariness moods.
Old despair attitudes.
Unjustified guilt feelings.
Adolescent death wishes.
Unnecessary habituated worries.

In any case, when life reaches a place in which you say you "can't go on," understand that you only mean (but do not know it) that you cannot go on in your present human relations and in your setting. Instead of taking your life, take a vacation. Go away from all the strain into an utterly new setting. Try Tahiti, or Samoa. Make friends with simple people and learn to play with the "jungle folk." The potential suicide is being told by nature that he has a right to happiness. He should take it.

Remember what Robert Louis Stevenson once said:

Anyone can carry his burden, however hard, until nightfall.
Anyone can do his work, however hard, for one day. Anyone
can live sweetly, patiently, lovingly, purely, till the sun goes
down. And this is all that life really means.

33   *Nerves on Edge*

You ask me why we are so sure fear of selfishness is
such a serious compromiser of life, why I insist that
freedom from this mass insanity is the key to most of
our life problems. I answer you that we draw our conclusions not only from knowing thousands of life stories
but from *testing methods* as well. Let me explain.

Many people have the idea that troubles have little
to do with one's mental life. They assume that one's
frame of mind plays no part in how difficulties are met.
Money problems are a matter of economics; business
problems are a question of trade relations; happiness in
the home depends upon food, clothing and shelter.
Just so. No one in his right mind will deny it. But when
this materialistic reasoning ignores the effect of a
person's frame of mind on the management of food,
clothing and shelter, or how he handles his home and his
money, the very heart of the question is misunderstood.

How you meet life is a matter of what you are—as
a thinker and doer. Any influence that injures your
morale must compromise your power. Most of the diffi-

culties we believe to be objective are essentially subjective and personal. Our greatest problem is with ourselves. Or, to put it another way: we must get the beam out of our own eyes before we can get the mote out of the life around us.

In these days thousands of people, when disturbed, seek the aid of psychologists. Let us imagine a typical conversation with a present-day consultant.

Mr. Gault is in a black mood. "I am very unhappy," he remarks. "I'm nervously fatigued. I don't sleep well. My doctor says there's nothing physically wrong. I have wondered if you couldn't get my wife and children to put less strain on me. I don't have any rest in my home."

"How long has this condition bothered you?' the psychologist asks.

"Oh, ever since I've been married," Gault answers.

To his surprise, instead of being questioned about his home, he is given a printed test to fill in. He is told to read each word thoughtfully and underline everything that at the time is causing him worry, anxiety or dread; and to indicate whether his response is weak, fairly strong, strong, intense, or one of actue anguish. This task completed, Gault hands the sheet to the psychologist, noting the special attention the man pays to the words marked "acute."

Mr. Gault had anguish about: fear, selfishness, evil, home, death, guilt, dreams, night, future, people, failure, poverty, regret, suicide, disgrace, memory, mistakes, weakness, depression, loneliness, nervousness, uncertainty, helplessness and discouragement. After a few minutes the psychologist turns to Gault:

"As a starting point," he says, "suppose we look over this list. There are words here that deal with all sorts of difficulties. You might, for instance, have underlined those that showed agitation over money, or your partners, the character of your wife, the neighbors, or friends. You could have disclosed embarrassment over social occasions. There might have been a record of sex discord, perhaps even a drink problem.

"Instead, you have indicated trouble about selfishness, guilt and death. You reveal feelings of insecurity, uncertainty and helplessness. There is marked anxiety about the future; you even fear suicide. This means your difficulty is not the pressure of your home life. Your trouble is in yourself. People blame present conditions for disturbances which haunt their inner lives."

It became clear that life was not so maladjusted to Gault as he to himself. The words to which he gave a negative response were only cues, keys to a fear of self with which they were associated.

It also appeared that Gault could not endure the smell of roses. Whenever he entered a room permeated by their fragrance, he trembled. At a dance, if he came into contact with rose powder or perfume, his face turned pale. He did not understand the emotional volcano created by the odor of this innocent flower until the consultant made a retrospective analysis.

Scrutinizing the case history, bit by bit it developed that Gault as a little boy had been taken to a hospital to see his mother before she was operated upon. Beside her on a table stood a bowl of fragrant roses. He was devotedly fond of her, yet his relationship with her was one of anguish. During her long illness his aunt told him he was "selfish" every time he made any noise. No one helped the little lad to find an outlet for his energies. "Bad, selfish boy" was all he heard. His mother died under the anesthetic. His feelings of guilt were those of a murderer. Roses were associated with this secret wound. They stood as symbols of his suffering.

Such mental twists distort our natural relation to life. There are millions struggling with their daily problems, whose minds carry such ancient hurts. The key to their troubles lies in gaining freedom at last from a blame that was unjustified. The curse of being called "selfish" is the cause of more failure than any other blight in life.

Of the many procedures used to reveal our ineffectualities, none is more telling than the one called *free association*. This is a method of bringing to the surface whatever brooding passions are most overpowering. It unveils the tumultuous centers surging under those surface reactions we call everyday experience.

Helen Hewett is attempting to use the process. She sits in the shadow of a passing day. Her eyes are following a bird on the skyline. Now and then she glances vaguely at the paper before her as she guides her pencil in a scrawled word association series. She is letting the last word written suggest the next word to her, just as a composer follows the inspiration of a melody. She writes: bird, cage, prison, home, beak, bird, mother, nasal, wrath, hate, horrid, west, door, light, horizon, safe lonely, Henry, dead, gone, empty, life, curse, mother, Oh God!

Need we go further into the bitter experience that is making a failure of this girl's life? From these words and their order, can we not unravel the story that Henry, the loved one, has been separated from his sweetheart by a nasal-voiced, sharp-beaked mother, sent away, gone West, become sick and died, leaving life empty, empty except for: "Come, Helen, it's time to get ready for Sunday school. Mrs. Jones will have her Ford at the door in no time. Put on that gray dress with the polka dots, it's more appropriate."

Isn't it amazing there are so few murders? And isn't it more amazing that we should judge present events without realizing how emotional conditions of the past deform our life-plots, shaping our thought and conduct in the here and now?

Has life failed Helen, or has her fear of herself and her moral terror caused imprisonment of normal impulses, making her fail life? But for the curse of that sanctified stupidity people call duty, might not life with Henry have been happy for Helen? Is her present relation to life what it would have been had she married him? Does she not see every daily difficulty through the mental distortions her experience caused? Has she not woven her reactions into her judgment? Wasn't her life ruined by fear of being wicked for wanting to marry Henry?

Along with this simple association process, other word tests are used to divulge our neurotic limitations. One known as the sentence association method is enlightening. The individual is told to take a relaxed position in a quiet room. As he gazes into space he lets himself go into subjective meditation, jotting down what his inner voice is saying. Out of what appears a hodgepodge of unrelated ideas, written without deliberate control, come betraying phrases and significant sentences.

Ben Andrews, a man of fifty, is in the throes of his masculine menopause, that tumult of emotion, so characteristically misunderstood. He is sitting by his window with a flickering candle on the table beside him. It is after midnight. The odor of new-mown hay comes through the trees. Rustle and restlessness are everywhere in the outer darkness.

Almost illegible words follow each other over the pad as feeling presses each sentence out. "My life is like this night: restless, tramping about inside. I cannot stop it. It is dark. It has been dark so long—the bank—the hours—hours there at the bank—like a vault—some cave in hell—dark—night—and only echoes. Life mocks me. Life has always mocked me. And love—bah! Let me lie down with crawling worms and the beasts of the field. Mahogany and the eight-thirty, and Flander's eating place. And Julia! Frowsy!"

Tomorrow he will start another day, that is, go through the motions. Somewhere in the past he moved off center; wrong home, wrong school, wrong friends, wrong job, wrong marriage; and now the burden of two senseless boys and a wife conspicuous for her manners and the absense of anything else. Could such a dirge make him anything but sick at heart?

Why does he stay in it? And why does he worry about present facts without seeking the causes that bring so many of them to pass? He is afraid of being selfish. His mind is obsessed by masses of negative imagery and distorted by abnormal attitudes.

Neurosis is a morbid compromise. The self is brooding and rebellious, afraid of its integrity. Its behavoir, however, is always self-centered, trespassing at every point against the edict: no ego satisfaction.

34   *Inside a Difficulty*

Henry Harding did not know what to do. He could, of course, resign. Several concerns wanted his services. He knew valuable formulas his company had spent years in perfecting. Competitors would give anything for that information.

But did he have a right to take such property along with him, even if he carried it all in his head? Wasn't it a matter of honor not to? He'd been trusted with those cherished secrets because his superiors believed in his integrity. Yet, how could he work for a rival firm and forget what he knew?

He couldn't, of course. Yet, he'd be expected to spend his time in perfecting manufacturing processes like those he remembered. How could he be fair to new employers? But was his company being fair to him? Here they were sending him and his family across the country without so much as a by your leave. He'd have to sell his house. It wasn't right.

All night, Henry lay awake, going round and round within his dilemma.

Modern science knows much about such conflicts. We call the mental state that engenders it "ambivalence": a collision between thought and feeling. Intellectually, Harding knew that the Intercontinental Dye Company had a perfect right to send him to California. He'd agreed to it, in fact, when he signed the contract on first being employed. He understood, too, that the change was in the nature of a promotion.

His reason understood and wanted to go. What he felt about it was another matter. All through his marriage, he'd never been far from his mother. He couldn't admit this to himself. He, a grown man with a family. To face the fact that an emotional fixation was holding him was impossible. Nor would he consider his timidity, his dependence on a familiar home setting and old friends.

Those troubled with self-doubt form a maze of indecision. It serves as a pacifier. They can then seem to be making mighty efforts to reason out their disturbances without doing anything that threatens their fears. "I can't go," Harding told himself one minute, and then: "But I must, of course," he decided the next.

Let us imagine that the next day the weary man sought the aid of a consultant trained in handling such problems. How would the expert proceed? Can we not picture him using what is called "the gimlet technique," a modern form of the Socratic method, questioning Harding to discover the cause of his stalemate? And would not two clear pictures have come to light?

A. The fact that the young engineer had received a natural and expected promotion and stood to gain in his career by the change, while in no serious way discommoding his wife and children.

B. The fact that he retreated emotionally from this transition for purely personal and somewhat neurotic reasons, and was clouding his thinking by the fog of emotionalism.

"You are the victim of at least a score of mental aberrations," the consultant would have said. "I'll list a few of them for you. This first is 'prior entry': a technical term for the establishment of a series of set ideas that invalidate your thinking. You gained beliefs as a boy about how you would live and work. They included staying near your parents. Next, you are guilty of what we call 'fusion.' You aren't thinking about this act of going West, in and for itself. You've mixed it all up with your feelings of homesickness. Every time you try to think about practical steps, an act known as 'unconscious shift' slides your attention over to the feelings of loneliness and dread about being away from your friends and the familiar setting.

"You've established a series of 'prompting centers,' like little phonographic disks in your brain. When you try to reason, these records begin to play. If I should take time to make a graph of your repetitive mental process, it would show an average error in your conclusions at the point where your rebellion starts: namely, anger against your superiors for separating you from your parents. I don't want to be too technical and scientific, yet you are an engineer and I hope to convince you that one can be quite as accurate and definite in analyzing mental problems as in engineering processes.

"Not once in your talk with me have you separated what we call the implicit facts, which you create in your emotional disturbance, from the explicit facts of the situation itself. Nor have you done anything to break your circular thinking and to consider what is the center of it. There's one clear fact you've never mentioned."

"And what is that?" questioned Harding, a little ruffled.

"That you have your living to earn," the consultant answered briefly.

"But I can get half a dozen other jobs," Harding shot back.

"You can?" the consultant raised his eyebrows. "I doubt it. Any competing company would wonder why you were changing so suddenly. If they took you, it would not be for your services, but for your secrets. You know that. How about your peace of mind? You have a conscience, I've discovered. Wouldn't you feel like a crook, knowing that your old company would understand just why a new position was so suddenly available?"

"You're right," muttered Harding. "No, I couldn't do it. I'd be in hell."

"I think you would. Now, instead of circling and circling, stick by this one central point: to work or not to work, that is the question. At least it's the question if you expect wages equal to what you've been offered."

"And you mean my emotional pull isn't as important as my job?" the engineer queried.

"Well, is it? Your wife wants to go. So do your children. Your parents won't die because you became weaned at last. It's part of growing up, this going West."

"You're right again," Harding answered, rising, "I'm going."

We speak of our troubles as if they were mainly economic. It is poverty of spirit more than of gold that
sullies our days. Even in dread of destitution, we suffer because we feel inadequate. Up to the time of seeing the
psychologist, Harding talked constantly of his troubles,
and thereby hid his own obliquities. He exhibited an
edginess characteristic of nervous people. His apprehension caused a contraction of his nature, as if he were
thrust into two personalities: one who fled from facing
facts, the other who sat like a critic and shamed him for
his fear. With the weakness of his hold on reality, he
had conceived abysmal pitfalls.

His timidity was known to few. They took the symptoms of his inner struggle to be the man himself. Even his
wife accepted these appearances and treated him ac-
cordingly. In her own way, she was as little revealed as
he, because of cataclysmic congestion within her,
which thwarted all attempts to solve life's problems. She
felt ostracized and numb. Her forlornness sprang only
from the paucity of her responsiveness to life, created
by doubt and self-consciousness.

Of all factors that deny a conquest of trouble, this emotional involvement in the mere process of living is the
worst. Because of it we become distracted and exhausted.
Statistics show that many of our industrial accidents
occur because of inner anxiety. At home, tension makes
your wife spill the cream; you burn your trousers when
lighting your pipe. In thinking, you no longer consider
what psychologists call "balancing factors."

In such a state you are advised to relax and let your
problem rest a while: to read a novel, go to the
theater, play cards, take up some social conversation, after you have done all you can. But what avails this counsel if you carry your troubles with you?

There are few who practice detachment, freeing
themselves from pressure, thinking about their problems

as if they belonged to someone else: putting them at a distance, seeing them in and for themselves. When sick with fatigue, you may fret about your business when the real issue lies in the wearied pondering. He who carries his bothers to bed is never free of pressure.

A major change comes to pass when one determines to conquer his psychic plagues. The wise man does not deny the hard facts of life, but admits his own turmoils.

In the relation of these two factors lies a confusing point in the analysis of human experience. Which of these causes our life troubles: neurotic inner conditions or bad outward circumstances? The answer is: *neither*. There is an apparent contradiction here that has upset the philosophies of nations and made the study of experience difficult. Putting the blame on personal abnormalities delays an evaluation of social evils. An accent on circumstantial wrongs creates misinterpretation of neurotic states. Sanity lies in seeing that each plays its part in our dilemmas.

We fumble fate when out of order, but fate is also quite as riddled with bad conditions. More than this, the mental attitudes which limit our power to conquer our troubles were created by the destructive effect of circumstance in the tenderer years.

The apparent dilemma is like that of the chick and the egg, except that we know which came first. Were society intelligently organized and home life free of moral decadence, there would be fewer neurotic ravagements.

Once an abnormality comes into being, however, it makes our relation to environment many times more difficult. Even in the best of circumstances, adjustment is hard. Thus it is that a man like Harding, having passed through experiences in infancy that bound him to his home, had seen his promotion as a threat instead of a victory.

In other words, under the blight of neurotic imagery, one does not see his problems clearly, but beholds them through the distortions of immaturity. Henry Harding's thinking had been compromised by the ego satisfaction he found in parasitical dependence.

35   Why Hardships Are So Hard

The conclusions it is my privilege to present in this book are based upon a study of the problems of one thousand men and women, chosen because their difficulties were typical. They were individuals like yourself, whose minds were bothered with the pressures life presents. Many of them were unhappy, but not more so than your husband, your wife, or your mother-in-law. Their troubles, too, were not unusual, the fears and worries noted were ordinary enough.

Thus in the records of these cases one finds marriage problems, dread of people and money troubles, melancholy, loneliness, cynicism and doubt of life. All these may center in one case, as well as self-indulgence, conflict, self-pity, sex disturbances, vocational maladjustment and fatigue. Difficulties with brothers, sisters, mothers-in-law, wrong partners, stupid employers and other secondary conditions appear, as well as the influences of wrong food, poor sleep, deficient glands and a thousand and one factors of early conditioning.

Recognition of these elements and their interaction is the foundation of practical psychology. A common-sense consultant seeks to understand what the data means. If it points to a serious misunderstanding of the "self" in the face of trouble, he can but record that fact. He does not create it. No ordinary, merely objective, troubles were recorded.

*Reasons for Seeking Psychological Aid
Discovered in 1000 Cases*

1. Loneliness, egocentricity, concern about self 849
2. Environmental problems, money troubles, financial insecurity 827
3. Self-indulgence, hedonism, conflict of necessity versus desire 621
4. Boredom, mentalism, rote-mindedness, cynicism about life 582
5. Indolence, parasitism, sometimes "drink" 527
6. Ethical uncertainty, involvement and anxiety 482
7. Nervous tension, fatigue over responsibilities 462
8. Self-consciousness, embarrassment, feeling of inadequacy, concern over people's opinions 428
9. Morbidness, martyrdom feeling, self-pity, blame 412
10. Sex difficulties, erotic disturbances, confusion over passions 396
11. Discouragement, blockage, frustration, bitterness about achievement 384
12. Ambivalence, uncertainty, worry over indecision 383
13. Emotional immaturity, mother complex, failure of independence 357
14. Stereotyped fixity, hyperliteralism, quandaries of conscience 352
15. Misunderstood, hypersensitivity, hurt by criticism .. 342
16. Dormancy, marked inhibition, torpid and unhappy .. 319
17. Nuclear complex, secretly homebound, unadjusted in life 316
18. Overadaptation, vacillation, purposelessness in contacts 303
19. Remorse, depression, melancholy, obsessed by guilt. 298
20. Oversophistication, futility, devoid of interests 271

21. Formless dread, anxiety, worry in general 245
22. Marriage problems, trouble over temperamental incompatibility . . . . : 243
23. Scattered mind, dissociation, unable to concentrate . . 219
24. Home conditions, parent problems, troubles with children 214
25. Vocational troubles, bothered over nature of work . . 210
26. Social problems, puzzled about human progress 197
27. Love problems, emotional immaturity, romantic disturbance 187
28. Nonadaptation, rebellion, difficulty with people 174
29. Nervous exhaustion, inner turmoil, anxious about health 138
30. Business pressure, nervous fatigue, daily problems . . 136
31. Nervous fear, insecurity, phobia, dread of dangers . . 126
32. Oppressive mothers, possessiveness, bothered over parents 124
33. Impulse-ridden, compulsion and discontent, in trouble over conduct 123
34. Hatred of civilization, contentious over conventional limitations 106
35. No meaning in life, doubt of immortality, or fear of death 102
36. Emotional immaturity, father complex, upset over independence 94
37. Hypochondria, imaginary health problems 88
38. Man fear or man hatred: androphobia, antagonistic toward other sex 79
39. Disliked and aloof, superiority, apprehension about position 76
40. Mother-in-law problems, vicariousness, bothered over parents-in-law 75
41. Suicidal impulse, cynicism, full of revenge 72
42. Censoriousness, perfection, guilty over secret lust . . 68
43. Woman fear, or woman hatred: gynophobia, dislike of other sex 68
44. Religious problems, puzzled about God 52
45. Dominating fathers, male arrogance, upset over parents 34
46. Homosexuality, obsessed by sex isolation 26

47. Business problems, enmities, injuries 14
48. Father-in-law problems, vicariousness upset over
    parents 12
49. Delinquency, temperamental maladjustment, fear of
    punishment 9
50. Stupidity, subnormality (moron), no worry at all .. 8

Our statement that most individuals are beset by more than one problem is well proven by this record. A single condition may dominate a man's thought, but in general we are troubled by what is known as a constellation, a group of particularly and peculiarly accented aberrations.

Ward Evans has emotional inferiority, sex neursathenia and money problems. His older brother shows evidence of superiority, a bad marriage situation and moods of melancholia. Millie Brandeis feels intellectually inferior but compensates for this by impulsive effort, which makes employment difficult. Her brother, Frank, has a mother complex that has now produced homosexuality and vocational uncertainty. Two of his friends are drink cases with periods of compulsion, and one of them, a college girl, has suicidal tendencies.

Unlike academic reports on laboratory research, these cases were not chosen at will. They were dealt with in clinical practice. Hence they are representative of everyday life. As the workshop was that of experience, the data could not be gathered with the same precision as that in the controlled examinations of laboratory research.

What burns into consciousness about this list is how deeply people are concerned with the dilemma of human relation. Nearly half the thousand felt themselves inferior to others. More than three hundred felt misunderstood and unfairly treated by their associates. A nearly equal number were in the throes of discouragement, boredom in intimacy, and felt that love had lost its savor. Eighty-four percent gave loneliness as the greatest ache in their hearts. With such unsatisfied longings it is small wonder that there are so many unhappy people.

Some hint of the situation comes with knowing that sixty-two percent of these people were so spoiled in babyhood that self-indulgence appeared as a dominant factor. They still sought from environment the enthronement of nursing-bottle days. Analysts are not far wrong in citing the nuclear complex—that is, the home and parent tie—as a mighty factor in neurotic states. Nor was Bergson mistaken in emphasizing the significance of such fixations.

The list shows a high percentage of indolence, that sighing of the soul for love without any adequate impulse to earn it. Here we have a cause of much adult difficulty, a crippling result of the parasitism fostered by weakly indulgent parents.

Psychoanalysts may object because neither sex, marriage nor love problems loom high in number. They will claim more were not reported because a Freudian technique was not used, and hence various erotic factors were not revealed. But if you add up all the ratings of love, sex, home and marriage difficulties, the total tops all others.

The total number of aberrations among the one thousand persons proved to be twelve thousand two hundred thirty (12,230), an average of a little over twelve phases of disturbance in every constellation. Some had but four or five tension centers, others eighteen or twenty, depending on the seriousness of their unhappiness. The neurotic drama is formed of a community of ideas, of grievances gathered into groups and superstitions organized into systems. We lug our longings into these arrangements as soon as circumstances irritate us.

It would seem, therefore, that most troubles, after we have become adult, do not reside so much in life as within ourselves. During childhood we were victims of our environment, of "mother love" and father platitudes. When we were spanked and sent to bed for a selfishness that was not wrong, there was nothing we could do but bear it. This fatal feeling, now that we have become further conditioned by the social order, is carried over as the cause of our present negative frames of mind.

More than ninety percent of the one thousand cases felt their lives seriously circumscribed. Of the few not obsessed by family domination and free from the pressure of being maried or unmarried (and unhappy because they were either married or unmarried) most felt that they lived among dull people and had little chance for joy. Some showed scant faith in life, were cynical and sad while admitting that they had hoped for perfect happiness. Many brought a dubious focus to the question of fidelity. The majority could underline things they hated in life, but few could give a satisfactory list of the things they loved.

It is a startling experience to discover from this assemblage that so many people are in a neurotic condition. It should prove that most of our troubles remain only because we are thus compromised. The difficulties may be in the external world, but we are the victims of them because of moods within ourselves.

In the last analysis, then, the trouble in these one thousand people was personal turmoil from the compromise of themselves, and a turbid unrest taking the form of unwise ego satisfactions. Instead of conquering experience and overcoming trouble, they lived uncooperatively, competitively, rebelliously, believing that the fate they experienced was destiny. Where mutual aid is lacking, luck is lacking also. Misfortune is mistress of our days.

To give up the delusion that husband, wife, mother, father, son, daughter, those on the job or in the neighborhood, are producing all our trouble, is a benefit beyond measure.

36   *Where Sorrow Ends*

Few of us wish to strive for peace. We want it spilled into our laps. We resist tearing into our complexes, in order to solve our other troubles. We wish our physic limitations removed—under ether, as it were. It seems unfair to ask us to exert any effort ourselves when circumstances are so hard.

It does no good to complain about it. If your mother dropped you when you were a baby: ergo, you were dropped. Your injuries are a fact. They must be dealt with whether the situation is fair or not. If, instead, she gave you a neurosis, that is also a fact. Unless you want to spend your days under the blight of psychic crippling, you have no choice but to give vigorous attention to correcting it.

People constantly ask: "How long does it require to come out of a neurotic condition?" And the answer is: "No one knows." Time is a delusion. Release from neurosis is slow or rapid according to the depth and thoroughness of your psychical state.

When you have a troublesome appendix, it is removed by modern surgery with but little suffering. If you have a stomachache you are given a pill. In the psychic realm there are no such anesthetized operations, and no such pellets. You are required to work on the removal of aberrations with the same fortitude one must possess to wrest a living from the soil.

There have been many definitions of neurosis. The best of all is to define it as the entrance of negativism into one's consciousness. The individual's thinking is colored by the darkness of doubt, made tumultuous by haunting dread and smothered anger. He tries to think, becomes morbid, and ends by feeling oppressed. His spirit knows frustration and is steeped in torpor. Sometimes in despair he forces his attention from his horror chamber, fleeing to excitement and pleasure. He involves himself desperately in his duties, coercing external activities to escape the inner pain.

No solution is found by thus forsaking the personal problem. No way out will present itself unless you go back to your inmost center and there wrestle with the demon of perversion. Stalemate develops otherwise.

There are, as you know, many who resist this fact because they fear it. They prefer to leave their minds alone, even if it means disaster. There is some justification for this point of view, for unquestionably there is danger in the analysis of neurosis, if constructive therapeutics are ignored. One must build good imagery in place of the negative attitudes, or despair may overcome the victim.

To meet this problem, my father used a technique in his practice, which I believe is superior to that employed by many in present-day clinical work. It was his custom, after a period in which he and his client sat for a while in utter silence, to begin a quiet, passive analysis of the person's frame of mind, seeking to penetrate what he called "negative atmospheres." This continued until some vital point was seen by the client. Then suddenly my father would change from the passive mood to an intensely active role. With swift strokes he built a positive picture to direct the person's thought along constructive lines.

This dynamic imagery was a vivid portrayal of what, but for the negative habits and interfering neurotic attitudes, his client would have followed in his life. My father never failed to associate the affirmative procedure so intimately with the negative moods that his client could not again sink into the old atmosphere without at once being brought to recall the brighter viewpoint. By the repetition of this means, a door was habituated out of the neurosis into a healthful frame of mind.

The method adjusts part after part of a person's nature which had formerly been bound by bad thinking. Each time the individual made contact with some abnormal feeling, he also recalled a new and positive focus that led to a better way of life.

If my readers will make it a rule to think out and intimately associate a healthful, dynamic behavior pattern with every unfortunate and destructive factor that is uncovered in their analysis of themselves, they can do more by this single control of attention than by all other procedures.

This technique is, in its essence, the art of using the very means to cure a condition by which the neurosis comes into being. Having discovered the "atmosphere" of one's aberration and the mode and imagery of which it was composed, one uses the very passion he found there to establish a constructive change.

This permits the second great process to come into play: go contrary to your complex. Act in the opposite way from that which you are inclined to follow because of your emotional sets and neurasthenic imagery. If you are shy and retreating, practice the art of being with people and taking part in their activities. If a mother complex suggests you stay in the home, go out of it and visit friends for long periods, or seek a position at some distance from your native setting. When fear restricts your sphere of action, insistently broaden it by an effort every day beyond the restricted boundaries. A mental state is broken up when we release power that has hitherto been suppressed.

If your mind is not in the best of order, if fears and tensions are apparent, this personal readjustment is also an essential step in many of your difficulties. The key to your marriage problem may be more within your own emotional state than in the unhappy situation itself. Your vocational difficulties, even the problem of employment, may come from an inner turmoil.

We in the atmosphere of the newer psychology receive a shock when meeting some old friend who still lives in the world of external values. He believes he sees what people are like and thinks there is no help for them.

One wishes such skeptics might witness the change that comes over those who have passed through therapeutic analysis. You may have had this experience and know how it feels to come alive. You may have tried to tell how differently things look: the trees greener, the sky brighter, the sun warmer; how people were kinder and all the earth smiled.

In the deepest sense, the cure of neurosis is a return of personality to its integrity, with the added assurance that it need not again submit to any compromise of itself. It is with equal force a return of personality to a cooperative spirit, freeing it from the blight of foolish and infantile ego satisfactions.

This does not mean that there are not continuing

difficulties, nor is the individual entirely free of the old condition. From sheer force of habit, it may still pull him for a time to the same old depths. But he comes back, and rarer and rarer is his loss of poise.

31   Secrets in Divorce

If you are an average American, particularly a woman, it didn't occur to you when love came into your life that divorce might enter also. Your romantic dream included no idea of love ending in dispute. You repeated: "Until death us do part," with full confidence in your vow. But being an average American, your chances of having a divorce are greater than any other danger in your life. In 1965 almost 400,000 American couples divorced in that year alone.

Even the accident rates in these days of crowded streets and fast driving are low compared with the figures on the collapse of wedlock. Out of every nine marriages two are likely to end in divorce. This number is mounting. Statistics show a two hundred and fifteen percent increase in less than half a century.

In 1910 there were twelve and four-hundredths percent of divorce. By 1930 it was twenty-one and seven-hundredths. By 1950 the figure had gone to twenty-five. It is easy to see why the experts fear a total collapse of marriage if the present rate keeps on.

The social danger of this situation is actually more serious than these legal figures show, for not half of the ruined marriages end in court action. Our confidence in love and the permanence of intimacy is shaken by the rarity of marital happiness.

It is not a simple question either. Suppose you are a woman with three children to take care of, ages four, six and nine. Your home, of course, is mortgaged, else you aren't in average circumstances. Or maybe you rent an apartment. In any case, money must be paid out to keep a roof over your head. You discover that your husband, who travels for a wholesale company, has lost interest in you. Is there another woman? You have no job, no visible means of support.

Are you in a simple situation in which love and its needs alone rule? By no means. Marriage, as now constituted, is as much a matter of economics as it is of psychology. Yet we cannot stop here because love is tied to daily bread. Any woman who thinks about it knows that no home is worth having unless her man chooses of his own free will to remain in it. Sickness, failure, death follow from enforced intimacy. Slavery by economics won't work.

So we are forced to surrender a lot of our prejudices and see what can be done when love fails and marriage goes to pieces.

Some time ago, I went to a banquet. A supreme court justice sat just across from me. We had eaten a delicious dinner and the ladies had left us.

"You psychologists are often critical of the way we judges handle marriage problems," he said. "What would you do differently if you sat on the bench?"

It was a direct challenge.

"I'd probably do no differently than you do," I answered, "for I'd be limited, as you are, by the customs of justice in America. We students of man's mind are not blaming you jurists as individuals. It is the general conduct of jurisprudence in relation to marriage we condemn."

"You mean that we judges, limited by tradition and the law, can't do justice to the individuals in a marriage tangle?" his honor asked in a gentler voice.

"I mean just that," I agreed. "I'm not blaming you men. Even in states where marriage laws are backward most judges are doing as much as their laws allow. It's the traditional legal attitudes, the disregard for the facts of life, love and human nature that seem to psychologists so unfortunate.

"I'd like to see our whole social point of view get into line with our scientific and engineering progress. Almost everywhere marriage is treated about as it was a hundred years ago. We aren't as backward in chemistry, mechanics, or," waving my hand toward the electric lights, "in illumination. I see no smoky torches here."

"Then how would you change the general procedures or, to put it better than that, what would you do as a divorce court judge if you were free to do what you deemed advisable, and the courts would permit you to carry out your ideas? First, second, third, now; what would you do?"

"First," I answered, accepting his categorical listing of my conclusions, "first I would view the situation as a surgeon does injured patients: as victims of social carelessness. Did you ever see a man or woman properly prepared for marriage; taught; I mean, to know what sort of mate to seek, or how to make the necessary adjustments to the personality of the mate?"

"No—no," his honor blinked, "I guess I never did."

"Then I would remove all blame from the individuals. They have suffered from the failure of society to teach them knowledge of human nature early enough in life so that their insight becomes as unconscious and automatic as their mother tongue. Those who seek a divorce are not at fault; we cannot hold them responsible until they know how to select a mate intelligently. Their divorce comes only as an inevitable consequence of ignorance." As I spoke, I began to pour water into my glass, stopping just as it was brimming full. "If I kept on, your honor, the water would slop over. Everything has its saturation point. People in unhappy marriages slop over when they can stand no more. I wouldn't condemn them. I would bring Christian ethics into the court and stand for the forgiveness for which Jesus pleaded."

"And you'd give them another show?"

"Certainly. In no other area of life do we hold the inhuman attitude that we do about marriage. If two men go into a partnership and fail to work in harmony, we say: 'They ought to break it up. They are injuring each other's success; they couldn't have known how it would work out.' There are horses who cannot be made to pull together. We would consider anyone mad who insisted on keeping them in double harness.

"That leads to my second point," I continued. "I would treat divorce as a necessary surgical operation to avoid the infections that would otherwise follow. Continuing an incompatible relationship is the worst thing parents can do to their children. One whole and peaceful parent is twenty times as good for a child as two quarreling personalities. Society may someday reach that sensible point of forbidding incompatible parents to remain together, so tragic are the effects of it upon the future citizen."

"What sort of any inquiry into the cause of the divorce would you advocate?" his honor asked.

"Not the sort of inquest now required by the court," I replied sharply. "I believe in the Scandinavian attitude toward divorce: that it should be granted at the request of either party without any consideration of so-called guilt. I've handled thousands of marriage problems, but I've never seen a triangle in my life. That's an illusion. No man or woman turns to a third party until something serious has happened in the marriage itself. True love is a closed corporation. As long as it exists, no one else can enter."

"I wonder if it has ever occurred to you that this question of divorce largely concerns women. Biologically, a man can step into and out of marriage with very little risk. Society seeks to equalize the situation. Marriage laws are to that end." The judge's voice was firm as he spoke.

"I grant that entirely. But we aren't mere creatures of biology—animals, if you will. We have minds, and insofar as we are human, divorce is a matter of psychology. Woman must be protected, as you say, but she's not much helped when a rebellious husband, who hates her, is forcibly kept in the relation."

"What about discipline?" the judge interjected.

"Discipline! Do you want young people to turn to free relations and indulge in general promiscuity?"

"No, certainly not."

"Then let's give up painting marriage as a hopelessly unpleasant relation, in which people suffer years of disappointment for the welfare of children and society. Do you know who causes the ways of wild youth that so many complain about?"

"No." His honor seemed anxious to find out.

"Those who preach that marriage is a duty, an abnegation of the self for the sancity of the home. They make it abhorrent to youth by destroying the idea that romantic love and sexual comfort can remain in marriage. I'd restore love to its true place. Marriage was not sanctified in the Christian Church until the Dark Ages. That is an historic fact. Until the period of greatest social and religious corruption, love was sanctified. I would restore it to its throne."

"Then you really wouldn't try to discover what led the couple to seek a divorce? You'd just grant it?"

"No. I wouldn't just grant it: that is, not until I had discovered what neurotic patterns were interfering with the success of the relation. Did you ever hear of mother fixations and inferiority complexes?"

"Certainly," his honor bridled, "everyone has nowadays."

"Well, a man who always compares his wife with his mother, and expects her to follow her every example, is fixated. He is emotionally sick, but doesn't know it. So is a woman whose sexual nature has become suppressed by prudery and the effect of a dominant father. And as for such conditions as inferiority complexes and hypersensitivity, they can ruin any marriage."

"Even naturally compatible ones?" the judge questioned.

"Yes, even relations that might be happy in the extreme. I once had to introduce a man and his wife to each other, though they had been together twelve years under the same roof. He had a mother fixation and a superiority complex. She was father-ridden and abased by the feeling of inferiority. They hadn't the least idea what each was like under the neurotic overlay. We are not ourselves when emotional fixations control us, and we don't act as we naturally would. People constantly judge each other by the condition they have gotten into."

"Isn't that natural?"

"No, it isn't. It is ignorant. If your boy has the measles, do you think of him as a measley boy?"

"No," the judge laughed.

"Well, I wouldn't think of a person with unconscious emotional fixations as the person any more than I'd call you a sniffly nature because you have a cold. I'd separate the person's character from his unfortunate habit formations, and I'd have a couple facing a divorce try to do the same thing in order to see if the trouble was unhappiness because of neurosis."

"And if they found that was a fact? What then?"

"If they were poor, I would send them to a public clinic; if well-to-do, I'd advise the aid of an expert in the cure of emotional abnormalities. After a year's try, if the attempt failed, I would grant the divorce. And let me tell you, we would have far fewer divorces if any such procedure were followed, and many more happy marriages."

38   *Two Sides of One Picture*

There are some problems about which no one should offer advice. If one did, one would trespass on the integrity of another mind. It is, in fact, a vital tenet of clinical psychology to *explain principles* rather than to *tell a person what to do*. Wisdom is never dictatorial.

Martha Merrifield was in a quandary: the problem of problems faced her. The man she loved was married. "Hopelessly married," she said, meaning that there seemed to be no solution.

What should she do? Her background was very strict. Her ancestors had walked on paths so straight their toes turned in. There came an afternoon in May when Martha felt she must settle once and for all the torment in her heart. Should she elope with Donald? There seemed no one but Betty Sue to talk with. Betty was a sphinx of reticence and loyalty.

"I can't answer your question, Martha," Betty looked at her steadily. "I can't even tell you what I'd do. Many women in America have had your problems. They've solved it according to their beliefs."

"You mean you can't help me?"

"You'd hate me or anyone who told you to go, or not to go, to the man you love. And anyway, if I said you shouldn't, you'd go most certainly, and if I thought you should, you'd be more doubtful than ever. Advice on the great steps of life only confuses us more."

"I've got to think it out alone, then?"

Betty nodded. "And if you actually *think*, looking into the future without letting your desires destroy your judgment, you won't be long knowing what to do. It's a matter of discovering your values, isn't it, and of knowing what quality of feeling you have?"

"I love him," Martha said simply.

"I know, dear, but there are a good many kinds of love. If you were sweet sixteen and he a lad in high school, you wouldn't have to think so hard to know how real your love is."

Here again the new ethics is speaking, a standard far harder than that of petty platitudes. What is the highest good? What is the quality of one's desire? How deep is the love?

The answer to Martha's problem is, after all: never compromise yourself. If love asks that, it is not love but lust. Her answer, too, lies in *no ego satisfactions*. Mutuality inheres in every true act. Integrity moves where affection is great. The strength of life and the depth of love are one.

Had she known how to do so, there were things Betty might have said to help Martha form her conclusion without actually telling her what to do. She could have seen how upset her friend was as to the "injury to the other woman" which her part in the situation created.

She might have helped Martha to mature beyond the place of feeling responsible for the experience that had come to her. She could have helped also to show her that it was not possible for the man she loved to make his wife happy merely by trying to do so. Never in all time has mechanics or volition made love real. Nor is there benefit to anyone from its sacrifice.

We do not know much about affection save as the craving for it is first felt within us and then is given to another. Mercy comes when experience has taught us the need for it. So, too, with generosity. He who denies himself in the end takes away the rights and hopes of all about him. Those who seek radiance bring it to others capable of feeling.

You can't make anyone happy unless he is able to respond. No matter what you do, he has no joy from your giving, except as he can receive. Nor can you take away any man's pain, except as he is ready to outgrow it. He is injured by your unctuous solicitude.

Someday we shall know that self-sacrifice is the first step in predatory living.

Never steal another person's trouble and call this thieving a virtue. You are just as dishonest to take the discipline he needs as to rob him of bread. Pain belongs to the man it purifies. Sorrow is a solvent of the soul. To get a difficulty away from its owner is psychic burglary.

Martha's duty, then, was only to be true to Martha. If her love was real, that was enough. If God is love, her devotion could not be wrong and be a real devotion.

We have a ghastly irreligion, an abysmal carnality, in our creeds about love. One might say again: this is either a chaos or a Cosmos. If it is a chaos, there is no such thing as evil, no basis of ethics, no reason we should not be savages. If morality is possible, if there is a Divine Order, if this is a Cosmos, what is right for one person cannot be wrong for another.

Martha could not hurt any woman by loving and even claiming her husband, if her love and his were true. She would set her supposed rival free from the curse of half-measure living. Betty, then, had touched the center of the problem when she said: "It's a matter of discovering your values, isn't it?" To know what quality of love was hers would have resolved Martha's dilemma.

The other side of this picture presented quite as livid a portrait of pain. Isabelle Blaine had known for months of her husband's affection for Martha, known and realized, too, the cause of the change in him. Something had gone wrong between her and Donald. It had happened gradually, but long before Martha had come into his life.

In her heart she admitted this fact. But most of the time a bitter agony, a surging jealousy made her forget it. Anger at "the other woman," anger that she was alive, consumed her bodily.

One of the maddest of man's delusions is his assumption that his experience is of his own choosing, and character of his own making. Events come to pass even as the self is born out of the womb of time. Nature is at work. Character and destiny are her handiwork. She gives us love and hate, jealousy and reverence. All that is ours is the power to choose which impulse we shall follow.

As with Martha, Isabelle's problem was one of integrity to herself, that of meeting this challenge to her life with beauty and strength. She could fill herself with hate, driving out the last remnants of love; she could allow her reverence for the possibilities of intimacy to become vindictive jealousy. Or she could seek the finer, higher solution of her dilemma. That she chose this better way spoke for her spiritual poise.

"Since this experience was possible only because my marriage was very sick," she told herself, "I will do all I can to make it well. I will accept this suffering as a sign from life that I must work for love, strive for beauty in intimacy if I wish to keep my marriage. It has been but a poor substitute for romance. I will try to make it real. And I can't allow jealousy to affect my actions. No matter how angry and envious I feel, no matter what vindictiveness broods in my heart, I won't let it come into my speech or color my decisions. I know that always brings ruin. It shall not ruin me."

From keeping this close check on her barbaric tendencies, guidance came to her and she saw how she could act constructively in her situation. "I'll do the very opposite of what my jealousy impels," she decided. And so, instead of letting her primitive impulse have sway, she decided to become Martha's friend. She made her acquaintance and cultivated her society. They became unusually close. The disturbing romance disappeared.

Such a situation is successfully handled sixty percent of the time when a fine and sturdy spirit is pursued. If the deflection is only a flirtation, it is broken up. If it is an honest mistake, both the husband and the "other woman" discover it. If it is a serious matter, all three find out how deep and true it is and the wisest course is followed—with decency.

There are always instances in which the new relationship supersedes the old one because there are always situations in which the marriage was not "cosmically true." The new, may be.

In this whole dilemma we are dealing with the deepest of human impulses, or ought to be. Love is not so simple and malleable as many suppose. Put it in prison and it dies. Restrict it and it turns into hate. Force it and it disappears. You cannot will love, nor even control it.

You can only guide its expression. It comes or it goes according to those qualities in life that invite it or deny its presence.

We know nowadays that the laws of attraction and repulsion are as absolute as those of gravitation. Some things and people cause a harmonious response, others arouse antagonism. It is not a matter of good or bad, right or wrong, but of sympathy or revulsion. You do or do not continue to respond as your affection or your hate grows. And this is because you and the other person are as you are.

One may destroy love's activity and create sorrow and turmoil. He may ignore its precepts and live in loneliness. He may follow and even guide its expression and achieve happiness. Love is more kindred to the tides and the lightning than to man's little ego.

He may receive it and know the depth of intense emotion. He may constrict its flow and exist at half measure. He may misuse its power, distorting it into lust and predatory desire. Love is not anyone's possession. It comes into him or goes out of him, quickening him or leaving him, much in the way life is received or disappears. Again and again man has set himself above nature, only to discover how puny he is in the face of the forces of life.

That is why we may legislate marriage, but cannot legislate love. Unless it comes and abides, wedlock is worse for everyone than no intimacy at all.

In such a situation, more than in any other problem in life, successful handling depends upon a full adherence to the basic laws of personality. If you compromise yourself in such a dilemma, all hope of peace is lost. If you fight the situation, indulging in ego satisfactions and angry threats, your trouble becomes mountainous. Only by holding harder than ever to the spirit of cooperation, and still seeking mutual aid, is there any hope at all.

In the last analysis, both partners in any marriage entered into it as free and equal members of the human race. If they wish to remain free and equal, no predatory parasitism is possible. There is a true conduct beyond anyone's individual wishes—that is the thing to find.

It is not how you or how I would be done by that matters, but what each must do in obedience to the will of life. A wise unselfishness is not a surrender of yourself to the wishes of anyone, but only to the best discoverable course of action.

39   *New Skills for Quarreling*

The setting is a mountain resort, to which Louise Godwin and her grandmother have gone. Michael Talbut, her fiancé, is with them. Louise has refused to go on a picnic to which Michael wants to take her. She wishes to go to a local dance. Each had good reasons for his desire, but neither will listen to the other, or stop to get his point of view. Both are so absorbed in putting their ideas over, they are quite unable to pay attention.

More than this, as they quarrel, each interrupts the other with yes-buts, each indulges in the most incomplete and biased types of thinking. Michael enumerates his reasons in favor of the picnic, failing, however, to say that he believes it is his duty to go, because his mother is to be there and will expect him.

Louise intuitively feels that the maternal influence is in the picture, but dares not mention it. So she talks excitedly about the fact that a certain wealthy financier is to be at the dance, a man Michael should meet. This makes Michael jealous and he says he doesn't want to meet him. Louise asserts he doesn't want to get on in the world so as to take care of her in comfort—and then the fat is in the fire.

Each is being personal, prideful, unfair, secretive and somewhat dishonest. As the quarrel progresses each feels ashamed, hates himself, but acts more and more as if he hated the other person. What should one do in such a situation? There are seven essential rules:

Seven Ways to Quarrel Effectively

1. Stop. Remain silent and listen until your opponent asks you to speak.
2. Suggest a bargain: that each be given a certain time—be it five or fifteen minutes—to speak. The other person is not to say a single word in response, only to listen during that time. Say your say fully.
3. Try to bring to the surface all the unmentioned and fear-ridden reasons that you could not face or mention while arguing.
4. Do your utmost to keep impersonal, both while listening and while speaking.
5. Set a time for each to respond to the other's statement, also with no interruption.
6. If there is then anything to argue about, go apart for one hour, to think quietly. Don't brood.
7. When alone, write down all the other person's points and consider them as honestly as you can.

It happened that Grandmother Godwin was a woman of common sense, and as fond of Michael as of Louise. At the height of their tussle, it occurred to the young man to seek an ally in the elderly woman.

Louise agreed to talk with her, being equally confident that her relative would give her cooperation.

But Grandmother Godwin was wise. She knew that only fools enter into a quarrel, and big fools at that. "Go apart and think," she said, "then come to me separately. If you are each willing to tell me first where you have been at fault in this discussion, I'm willing to help you both."

We need not follow the gentle way she led these young egotists to see their attempt to dominate each other, or how she got them to discover that nothing was as important as their keeping in harmony.

"Why not a third plan?" she suggested. "Wouldn't you have just as much fun if you went sailing together?"

"I'd really like that best," Michael agreed, secretly glad he didn't have to yield, either to his mother or to Louise.

"I think that would be great," Louise consented, quite as happy over the outcome.

The principle of the third way, the undiscussed answer, the wise new adaptation. Remember it. It's a priceless solution of arguments.

There is more to the matter than this, however, and when by yourself it is well to see if you make some of the following mistakes. Do you:

Refuse to give the other person time to present his whole point?

Fail to admit it to the other person when he has convinced you of something?

Indulge in a great deal of titting for tat?

Bring irrelevancies into an argument when it is going against you?

Find fault with ideas because they emotionally upset you, thus refusing to be reasonable?

Lose track of what you were saying because of your suppressed anger, and then go on and on talking to cover up your diffusion?

Try to put things over without first thinking them out clearly so that you understand them yourself?

It is important to remember that you can't see ten points at once. If, in striving to be brilliant, you jump like an intellectual flea all about an idea, discussing first one then another point, you waste years learning the lessons of an hour.

Form the habit of saying to yourself: "Well, after all, what are the facts?" Restate them. Give the points in the argument a "true-false" analysis. Underneath most manifest statements are the latent motives and implicit forces, deceiving everyone and causing most of the difficulty.

For example, Michael was an average young man, yet he quarreled because he was contentious toward everyone as a result of his older brother's teasing. Louise had quite a little phobia, and had really resisted going on a picnic up a mountain because she hated high cliffs. A little honest self-facing, a little deep analysis done with loving sympathy to find the true facts, and great would have been the change.

Most of the time in arguments we project our own neurotic values on our intimates, charging them with our mental failure and obscuring the issue by trite phrases.

Some of the common blame patterns are worth considering. You accuse or feel blamed:

Because you don't agree with the other person, or he with you.
Because of following deep convictions.
Because of breaking the decadent moralities.
Because of undeclared ideals.
Because of native impulses.

Because you can't "do it" at the moment.
Because of your activity level, your rate of thinking.
Because your nature and interests are different.
Because of your deeply held principles.
Because you were born as you are.
Because you need to think things out.
Because of your divergent needs.
Because of inner longing.
For having greater or lesser abilities.
Because of ill fortune and its consequences.
To satisfy your ego, thinking everyone at fault except yourself.

Contentious men squabble at nothing and that is what they win. List the outcomes of fifteen of your quarrels. Weren't they fruitless victories?

Why not learn how to win by yielding? Here are twenty-four suggestions:

Clarify your purpose and keep it always as your aim.
Ignor every challenge that does not threaten your intention.
Give up in all nonessentials.
Keep the discussion to the things you are willing to surrender.
Return again and again to the points you will yield on.
Say nothing about your fundamental purposes, hold on and wait.

In the meantime, the quieter you are, the more powerful will you be. Some things to disregard as not worth bothering about:

Most criticisms and blames.
People's accidental mistakes.
All slights, whether intended or not.
All behavior that comes from ignorance.
All conduct from inefficiency.
All the ways neurotic people act.

All advice when impatiently offered.
All unsolicited obligations.
All mistakes no one can correct.
Most consequences of temperamental differences.
The unavoidable losses in life.
The imperfections of everyone.
The fact that life is full of troubles, and so is the situation you are arguing about.

In any case, pause in any discussion to put yourself at ease. Here are the rules of an old New England farmer:

Find something friendly and humorous to say.
Sit down in an informal and comfortable way.
Do some little act of courtesy.
Sit and meditate about the largeness of the sky.
Decide you aren't important enough to be defensive.

It has been well said that "if you win an argument, you lose a friend." You can't talk your associates into any worthwhile cooperation. One might paraphrase this: When you win an argument, you lose an end—the end you were seeking when you allowed the contention to deflect your purposes. Winners of disagreements become so exhausted by the wordy discussion they have little heart to fulfill their intentions.

A laugh is better than any blow. It strikes harder to boot. When it rings out in a quarrel, something happens to the morale of vengefulness. It becomes confused and inept in the face of gaiety. Learn to chuckle your enmities away. Arguments and crossword puzzles are matters of amusement. Keep them so. Teach yourself to treat any debate as play. Keep it light, full of humor and tolerance. The moment anyone you are talking with becomes personal or impatient, leave the room. Evacuation and irritability are private matters, and should so remain.

After all, if you do not indulge in ego satisfactions, you won't quarrel. Unless you refuse all compromise, you'll never keep your head. Only by balancing the impulse for personal integrity with that of mutual aid are intelligence and cooperation maintained.

40   Why Die Young?

Evans Strickland frowned. The interview was not to his liking. He had been nervous of late and, taking advantage of the presence in America of a famous French specialist, was seeking help. The years as a corporation lawyer in the turmoil of New York had taken their toll.

"It's hard work," he had told his wife. "No man can stand the pressure for long."

But when the great doctor told him the same thing, he was offended. He had hoped the man could "put him right" so he could go on living a life against nature. The consultant had no such magic.

"I've got to keep on, Doctor," Strickland explained, "but my nerves are all shot. I can't sleep. My head is foggy, my heart—"

"Yes, yes," the doctor nodded, "I quite understand. You Americans move so fast. You jump in four ways at once—and the heart, it gets to jumping with you."

Strickland allowed himself to be examined. "But I've been taking care of myself, Doctor. I know what to do."

"What is it that you are doing in this great caretaking?" the doctor demanded.

"Why, I've had lots of colds lately, and some constipation. I've been pretty tired, feel the dampness a lot. So I keep out of drafts, stay in bed Sunday mornings, take enemas regularly and dose up if I'm sniffly."

"And your stomach—does it bother you?" the doctor smiled.

"But I use the stuff for acid and all that." Strickland was defensive.

"Do you also use leeches and incantations?" the doctor asked mildly.

"What for?" grunted his patient, sensing what was coming.

"They would surely help. You let the body get logy, you do not exercise. You do not ever fill the lungs. You're out till midnight, or else stay home thinking you're resting; sitting like a fungus on a log. And then methods of a hundred years ago might have kept you in order—a hundred years ago. Now, you need your glands toned up. You must eat the right vitamins. Those are modern ways. You also need to avoid strain, to rest your nerves and not keep cooking your brain."

"Cooking my brain!"

"Yes, did you ever see an egg slightly boiled, when the transparent part is just turning white? That is coagulation at work. When you become exhausted and toxic and have no oxygen in the blood, the brain begins to coagulate. You are then just a bit insane."

Strickland caught the twinkle in the doctor's eyes and heard his chuckle, but it didn't assuage his anxiety.

"You mean I'm sometimes out of my mind?" he demanded nervously.

"Everybody when he's overtired is just a little touched. But the foolishness passes—that is, if one gets rested. Why do you have to work so hard?"

"My family needs the money."

"And how about the late nights?"

"My wife says that's the only social life we have together."

"You must get her to see your strain."

"I can't, Doctor. I don't want to be selfish."

"That wouldn't be selfish, only wise. You had a breakdown years ago, you tell me. Your behavior cannot be constantly injurious without damaging your nerves."

In other words, one cannot play bridge until midnight, cavorting about madly; then rush to his office in the morning, wheeling and dealing with glee; then drive like a demon to the country, flirting with death on a crowded highway; or spend without stint to build up social contacts. He cannot destroy every aspect of his life with a frenzied spirit of chance, and then hope that a breakdown will not follow.

He who no longer compromises himself, will no longer exhaust himself. Where strain is, he refuses to be. Nor will he for the ends of ego satisfaction indulge his whim at his body's cost. He who respects his nerve, also respects his nerves.

Strickland, convinced that the doctor could help him, began using sunlamps, doing exercises, eating the right food and having his endocrine system set right. But he also changed his way of living. The doctor gave him a few homely truths about the art of keeping well: a little of what modern science knows about brain fag.

Five Ways to Avoid Brain Fatigue

It is caused by an undersupply of blood to the brain, created by undue tension that acts on the body like a tourniquet. Stop your overeffort, overimmediacy, overconcern, overadaptation, and breathe deeply for three minutes every time you find yourself tense.

It is caused because people don't stop to get the guidance of their instincts and deeper judgments. Wait—wait a moment before action and give yourself time to think.

It is caused by conflict, by a confusion of purposes, by the tension of opposing ideas. Stop—write down the pros and cons, see which makes the stronger list. Act on the evidences of that list.

It is caused by toxic poison. Don't hurry your meals. Don't scurry after meals.

It is caused by the need of oxygen. When your problems are difficult, go to the window every so often. Your brain, like the motor in your car, needs air.

When you "can't rest," don't try to. Think of whatever most absorbs you. Seek the way you can safely and comfortably forget yourself. Then do it.

If you must travel so fast, you should have traffic lights to avoid a smashup at the crossroads of thought. Establish them, at fifteen-minute intervals. Stretch a little, rest a minute. Make this an absolute habit.

Did you ever watch a good horse, or a wise donkey, going up a trail? He halts every so often. Nor does he move again until his wind is restored. Unless you make this a practice of yours, you cannot expect to maintain the health of an ass.

Mrs. Durston couldn't sleep. She "hadn't slept in years." As soon as the light was out, the nignags of her day tramped about in her brain.

Her tasks seemed never done. Meals came around with irritating regularity. She wanted to read the new books, but never got around to it. Her mind was getting dull. Her husband thought her as unreasonable as her mother—a pretty strong way of putting it.

"But I'm always tired, George," his wife told him. "I feel distracted with so many things to attend to."

"Do them if you can; if you can't, let them go," George grunted.

"But I only do my duty. I'm not like that Mrs. Tage. Would you like to eat the kind of meals she serves?"

"No," shouted George, his attention aroused. "But that doesn't mean you need to cook them in your dreams."

"It's the details," sighed his wife.

"Isn't my business full of them?" George challenged. "Suppose we spent half an hour at this task and half at that. Where'd we be?"

"Yes, but your business is organized with filing systems and that sort of thing."

"Then organize your life. You haven't touched your

paino in months. Lots of things you do are unnecessary."

"You wouldn't have me leave my house dirty!" cried Mrs. Durston with feminine horror.

"No, but I wouldn't have you be a slave. Get some system."

Applying this advice, Mrs. Durston was amazed to discover that her disorderly "self-sacrifice" had been unnecessary. It surprised her more that she began to sleep.

Had she always believed in never compromising herself, she would not have let the details of her home interfere with her living. Now would that sense of persecution so common to domesticated women have allowed her to make responsibilities so great an ego satisfaction that it enabled her to enjoy the ill health of a weary and sleepless existence.

People troubled with insomnia are sick: that is, neurotic. Most of them are the victims of quasi unselfishness. All of them are being deprived of necessary rest. Good, sound sleep, sleep that continues until you are refreshed, is an essential psychical rehabilitation.

Recent studies of sleep teach us that physical relaxation rebuilds the body, but the psychic structure is also repaired by the somnolent state. The mystics assure us that in sleep our spirits are in contact with "the other world," and are nourished by an increased influx of celestial energy. Be that as it may, deep drowsing is essential to success. It is a primary and essential selfishness.

Unless you sleep well and easily, you may need to make a ceremony of going to bed. During my lecture season, I often have to sleep night after night on Pullman trains after hard days of speaking and handshaking. If I could not sleep, how long would I last?

I have taught myself to be a train sleeper. If my

methods work on a noisy Pullman, they can put you into slumberland on your soft bed.

If you find it a little difficult to sleep, use three or four of these methods. If harder yet, five or six. If you are a chronic insomniac, use them all. I have never known them to fail *when and if* faithfully applied.

Eight Ways to Assure Sleep

1. *Drink a glass of something hot.* Several products on the market that are advertised to make you sleep are nearly as good as a glass of warm milk. Did you not know you have a sleep association with milk? "Why, baby dear, you've had your bottle, now go to sleep and mother will sing." As you take your warm drink, reestablish the habit pattern of that first happy year.

2. *The body rub.* Start with your head and massage your scalp. Dig your fingers into the base of your spine. Then rub your neck and stretch it by trying to pull your head off. Do not jerk it; pull gently and not too hard, using only one hand on the back of your head. Next, rub your shoulders. Now knead your stomach; shake the old bag a bit, and as you do so imagine how the gastric juices are swishing about. Feel like resting yet? If so, stop and go to sleep. If not, double your fists up under the hollow of your back and jounce up and down to loosen your spine. Now rub your hips and thighs, and then those tired feet.

3. *Sighing, yawning exercise.* When going to sleep, babies gurgle, chuckle, murmur and sing. Birds croon; all animals, except fool humans, do something of the sort. Start sighing quite regularly. Then yawn. Every now and then snicker at yourself for your absurdly stiff tension. Feel the bed; it's grand. Sigh some more. Open your mouth and yawn until your ears crack. If you cannot yawn automatically, make yourself do it deliberately.

4. *Stretching and turning exercise.* Stretch and twist in every direction. Turn over on your knees, placing your chest on the bed. Now turn over on your back; stretch again. Wiggle all over; kick your feet. If you are married and sleep in a dou-

ble bed, go to bed first and thrash about until your nerves are satisfied. Then sing out to your partner that you will be quiet.

5. *The gentle eye pressure.* Press ever so gently on your eyes; lids closed, of course. Bear down on your eyeballs until they feel the weight of your fingers. Now let the pressure up ever so slowly and rub all about your eyes.

6. *Have a pleasant dream.* If you already have a dream that is especially attractive, use it. If not, pick out the most lulling, languid, luscious, lazy loveland you can imagine; a South Sea beach on a moonlit night perhaps. Go there in fancy, and dream about how you would feel. Float on the salty waves. Smell the flowers. The rest of your dream should be quite personal and private. Use the same dream every night. You never heard of a Brushwood Boy who had insomnia. It is nonsense, this idea you cannot sleep. You can, if you have a dream to go to, and are not afraid of a little harmless joy.

7. *Try breathing.* If you are still so stubborn as to be awake after floating on a somnolent sea, begin to breathe deeply; long, slow breaths through your nose. Not too long, just heavy, sleeping breaths that sound like the sea breaking on the sandy shore. Lie and listen to the waves, listen, listen, listen—until you are sleeping like a child.

The next exercise is only for very obstinate people, those contentious cusses, who like to prove no one's method will work. They must be willing to work themselves, however, to use it.

8. *Psychic deafness.* Make a mental image of being unable to hear. Think deep into the center of your head. Say to yourself: "I'm hanging up the telephone. I'm shutting off the radio. I'm not going to hear anything more." Repeat this process. Surrender to it. Practice it every night for thirty nights. Do not expect it to take effect the first sleepless night you have, for if your unconscious refuses to sleep, it will require discipline to conquer it. In about a month, however, you will learn how to close your ears and sleep.

In order to sleep well at night, remember that during the day you must spend less energy than you generate. Keep within your margin of strength. It isn't your duty to kill yourself by striving. It's only foolish unselfishness that makes you do it. A bankrupt body is worse than an empty bank.

Insist on eliminating worry reveries before going to sleep. If your problems aren't solved, go to your home library or den and sit until you have them thought out. Bed-wetting and bed-brooding are both infantile. You need to be mentally, as well as physically, "housebroken."

42   *In Sickness and Health*

Excerpt from the letter of a physician:

"One thing that needs to be understood by the public these days is the difference between an organic and a functional disease. It is not surprising, however, that this distinction eludes them; there are plenty of doctors to whom the two are not always clear.

"There is an important line, too, between those actual sicknesses of nerves and glands and the disturbances that are purely imaginary. A mental state shades so imperceptibly into a somatic one that many times the question of good morale is more important than good medicine. There was much to be said for the efficiency of the old-fashioned family doctor, who knew his patients so well that, because of his years of familiarity with their ways, he could diagnose their ailments with accuracy.

"More than this, when he came to a sickbed with his

friendly smile and his cheerful manner, his sympathy gave courage and confidence to his people. We may laugh at faith cures all we wish, but when we remove the constructive power of affectionate suggestion from our methods of healing, half the potency of medicine is gone. No matter how efficient the machinery and how expert the work of the specialists who handle sickness, nothing takes the place of confidence."

These are important words for anyone concerned with the problem of physical health, whether his worry is over himself or a member of his family. No one should underestimate the miracle of modern medicine, or its amazing development of instruments for the protection of health. But we do need to emphasize the points that this wise doctor so clearly presents.

When sickness is in the home, your desire is to conquer it. What sort of situation are you contending with, and what will be the effect of what you do and say upon the patient? Every doctor has seen hundreds of cases in which a nervous and hysterical member of a family has done more to make a sickness dangerous than a dozen physicians could do to get the person well. Keep the Aunty Dolefuls and the Gloomy Gusses away.

From years of contact with some of the finer of our American physicians, I would caution you to avoid the following mistakes when anyone is sick:

Don't resist expert advice until it is too late, and then rush madly to find help.

Don't take up with fanatical methods of cure and then condemn all medicine when these fail.

Don't believe a lot of old wives' tales about a sickness. There are plenty of ancient and foolish superstitions still at large.

Don't forget that physical hygiene in sickness is more important than in states of health. What a patient eats is often the determining factor. Your doctor knows more than your cook.

The right frame of mind is as important as the right physical care. If the house becomes a riot or a gloomy cave after the doctor leaves, his medicine hasn't a chance.

Most physical conditions have their mental and emotional aspects. Those called functional, especially so. The old "nervous prostration," colitis, and a score of such disturbances are largely dependent upon mental attitudes for cure. Listen to, and take to heart, your doctor's words as well as his medicine.

If he tells you there is a good deal of hypochondria in the condition, don't get angry and seek another physician. Thousands keep themselves sick by fears and negative attitudes.

Be sure you aren't being sick in order to gain attention. It's an indoor sport in America.

Picture a situation like this: Mary Staunton lies in bed with colitis. Dr. Vance is talking with Mary's mother, trying to get her to see how Mary is kept upset by the way her mother plays up to the young woman's self-pity and desire for enthronement. Dr. Vance insists that Mary has formed the habit of expecting everything to disturb her. She has acquired the attitude of disease.

"Your sister is a Christian Scientist, I believe?" he asks tentatively.

"Yes, why do you ask?"

"I was thinking of sending your daughter over there for a while," the physician answers shrewdly.

"Why, Dr. Vance, what an idea!" Mrs. Staunton is horrified. "Whatever would you do that for?"

"So she could have the influence of those who refuse to identify with ill health. I don't deny matter of germs, and all the rest of the somatic factors, but I'd like to see you hold your sister's optimistic attitude."

That's an important point in the question of health. Discover your food allergies, but don't make a fetish out of them. Correct your constipation, don't worship it. Do everything to cure your pain, don't live in perpetual fear of it. Cope with contagion, don't let it become a terror.

If it is you yourself who are sick, make a campaign for getting well. Ask your physician for ten ways of keeping yourself relaxed, your breathing deep and calm, your attitude optimistic. Ask him to help you focus your attention on the steps toward health. The average doctor will tell you twice as much that is helpful, if you assure him you want to know it.

The interaction of the mind on the body and the body on the mind is important indeed. Don't make yourself worse by worrying about anything or anybody while ill. That is your time to let go. Don't suppose you are actually as sad as many sicknesses make you feel; some of them cause temporary melancholia. Refuse to act depressed and you won't be half as miserable.

Talk to yourself calmly and wisely. Make autosuggestions of the ways you intend to get well. See yourself becoming better constantly. The only way to beat any sickness is with the attitude of health. Discover ways you can strengthen weaknesses in your morale. Have the room you are in made cheerful.

And remember, when it's someone else who is sick, that negative sympathy is poison. Never talk about anything morbid, least of all the dangers and sorrows of a person's condition, in his presence.

And this is quite as imperative when the condition is organic, caused by injuries, infections, contagions, germs, as when nerves and glands have caused functional states. Faith, fortitude and a little touch of fun are half of any cure.

It's a strange fact, too, that those who feel the urge of accomplishment seldom get sick. It may be that the very healthfulness of their relation to life protects them. One seldom compromises himself when his purposes are important. He has no time for the ego satisfactions of sickness.

43   *When Worried About Money*

Years ago, that great reproducer of the songs of birds, Charles Kellogg, proved by a neat experiment that our national consciousness is fixed on money. Insisting that each of us hears only what his attention is tuned to, and that we ignore scores of sounds that do not concern us, he tossed a dime to the sidewalk in a noisy street. Pedestrians stood still, their eyes searching for the coin. He himself, on the other hand, was able to hear a cricket singing in a cellar when no one with him could detect the chirp above the roar of traffic.

When a man tells you he is anxious about money, he does not mean what he says. He is afraid he cannot secure the things money will buy. If he were sure of his power, he would gladly be rid of the nuisance.

Let us picture one of those occasions when you are over-worked, have a cold, feel mean all over. Bed is full of granite ridges. You try to sleep. Your eyes won't close; they see envelopes on the table.

"Bills, bills," you growl. "Why can't they leave a fellow alone when he's sick?"

You lie there thinking about the cost of merely existing; that's all you do. Your routine isn't edifying. It's all very well for old Dr. Abbington to talk about your resting and threatening you with pneumonia if you don't. There'll be a bill from him pretty soon. A hundred dollars for medical services and time lost while you are convalescent.

As if to punctuate your complaint, Abbington enters on his afternoon round. Your pulse is counted, the temperature taken, the fussing done that leaves you in a rage. This afternoon, instead of hurrying away, the old gentleman sits down.

"Have you any special requests, funeral arrangements or that sort of thing, my boy?" he asks.

You sit up startled. "Don't you think I'm getting better, Doctor?"

"Yes, unfortunately, you're getting well fast, too fast for your ultimate good. That's why I'm talking to you. If you'd had to stay here a few weeks, you'd have been forced to take a rest. As it is, you'll be back in high speed in a day or so. But you can't keep it up, not and live very long. You've got to slow down. Why not let your junior partner carry more work?"

"Yes, and make the money for it I need. Half my sickness is money pressure, Doctor. Look at those bills. I've got to pay 'em, but I don't know how."

"You also don't know how to live, and that's the real trouble. You spend twice what you need to."

"Tell that to Millie, won't you?" you snort.

"I won't. That's your job, but not unless you do it intelligently. It's not Millie's fault. The trouble traces back to you."

For an hour the old doctor talks. What sort of budget do you have? How is the family organized to get the most within its income? How much do your children know about the cost of living? What part is each of the family taking in guarding against unnecessary expense? He finds you resistant.

"Your ego is involved in this matter," he insists. "You don't want to put your financial house in order. It hurts your pride. You'd rather feel lavish—and fuss. But it's no way to live. That's the American pattern, and the reason thousands of men die in middle life. I'm not suggesting a Scotch thrift, although it's infinitely to be preferred to what you're doing. I'm only insisting that since you worry about finances, you do something about your money problems. If pressure weren't killing you, it would be none of my business what you did. As it is, my counsel is better than my medicine. A family is a democracy, or should be. I'm only asking you to become reasonably intelligent in applying ideas with which you are perfectly familiar. Look here, I've one more suggestion, and if that isn't acceptable, I'll keep still and let you kill yourself. Would you be willing to call a meeting of Yourself, Wife and Children, Incorporated, and lay out this problem of expense and your health?"

"It sounds pretty selfish to dump all my troubles on my family," you object.

"Well, if it's selfish, it's a good deal more sensible than dying unselfishly and leaving them without your support."

"How'd you have me conduct this affair?"

"You sound as if you didn't know whether or not you wanted to do it. But I'll answer you anyway. When you are all gathered around a table, ask each one of your family to list the necessary monthly expenses."

"My children too, you mean?"

"Why not? How will they ever gain an idea of income and outgo if you never give them a chance? Combine the lists the four of you make and then put them in the order of greatest importance. Strike the last ten items off as being inadvisable just at present, or let the family vote on what seems essential after discussing it."

I know of a good many instances in which this plan has worked. If this country is to remain a democracy, the method of self-government should begin in the home. Thousands of wives, millions of children, have no idea of the facts of family income. In nine cases out of ten, an open discussion changes the outlook. It even affects the attitude of the man of the house, and helps him to balance income and outgo more successfully.

As long as any one of your fellow citizens can exist on a fourth of your income, you can budget your finances to avoid worry. We no longer live in fear of salvery, nor of descending Goths. The wolf howls at the door only as a figure of speech. But we aren't free of financial neurosis.

American money madness, as so many doctors know, is responsible for the high blood pressure which is so prevalent among men. The causes of this American disease in the mass are connected with our striving for wealth. Through that, the Americans have more or less lost the art of living. We have created false standards and deprived ourselves of peace and leisure.

One thing is certain. Money becomes a blight when we compromise ourselves for its acquirement. There is, in fact, no worse ego satisfaction than to seek riches and lose yourself.

I have an Italian furnaceman. He and his wife and children lived for some months on the pittance earned from shaking down my heater. Now, times are better.

I have a neighbor who heads a great corporation. He spends lavishly, but earns more than he uses for his luxuries. He considers the matter of his savings.

You and I, who don't like the size of our taxes and feel the rising costs of everything, still think about the time our earnings may fall below our present style of life. We need to protect our savings.

At one time, I supposed it was the wise thing to seek "expert" financial advice. I sought counsel from a conservative banker. He suggested I purchase a certain stock. Being a cautious man, I also asked the investment counsel in a large trust company. He advised the same. Then I consulted a personal friend with a seat on the stock exchange. He confirmed this advice. I now have six hundred shares of this stock. It's for sale for two cents for the lot.

If I were giving an opinion on the question of investments, I would start by saying: "Never accept the advice of a banker, an investment counselor or a broker. Seek their opinions, but get the judgment of practical men." I've checked on that statement for eight years in the affairs of countless people as well as in my own concerns; I know it is sound. One who handles money mainly can't seem to think except in money terms. That is no way to reason about finances.

Money isn't anything in itself. It stand for something. Your thought should be on what it stands for. We are certainly passing through a social transition. Labor unrest is increasing.

A conservative adviser in your bank may not believe what can happen in life. But it *can,* just the same.

What is the key to your problem, then? Efficient selfishness? Surely, if by this you mean using your own head. There are six general forms of investment:

1. Real estate
2. Goods and foods
3. Savings banks and insurance
4. Stocks and bonds
5. Private enterprises
6. Government securities

There are three ways of placing your money.

1. Speculatively: on margin.
2. Spec-invest: that is, fully held.
3. Permanently: straight saving.

Which way you choose depends on how important your need for protection is. Consider the change Peter Pawling has made in his investment policy. He used to play the market. He didn't take risks, but intended to get rich by taking advantage of the rising values. He kept on until the market dropped.

Now Peter Pawling has changed his ways. He believes a man's investment method should suit his income, his obligations and the circumstances of his country and its industrial stability. He has:

1. A little piece of real estate in a low-tax region.
2. Some goods and foods stored against rising prices.
3. A little money in the savings bank.
4. A few conservative stocks.
5. A bit of money in a conservatively run private enterprise.
6. A few government bonds.

What is the result? His worry has fallen so strikingly that he's worth twice as much to his company; hence, his salary has been raised.

Years ago, a financial adviser remarked: "Worry over investment is a sign that distribution is not sufficient." These are words of wisdom. If you are disturbed about savings, take it for granted you have not invested wisely. The diversification you have may be good in itself, but not as far as your state of mind is concerned. Someone might be a good adviser regarding your investments, but not so in view of your personality. Satisfy your unconscious feelings as well as your reason.

Psychic tensions spread unless deliberately limited. Half the marriage quarrels and many parent difficulties come from nervous fatigue engendered by economic pressure. See this; admit it. Set a time for concern over finances. Let your fears come up. See them. Talk them over with loved ones. Then close the door on them. Don't let them seep into your intimate life.

Get a few of your friends to tell you about their money troubles. Make a study of such matters. Listen to their woes until you feel a little nauseated. When you reach your saturation point, turn your attention to the act of living.

The solution of many a tension consists in giving up one's excited focus and looking in an opposite direction. Dan Sterling gave up brooding about the money people owed him when he said to himself: "It does no good

for me to fret about it. I'll think how I can help my
debtors to pay me."

He laid out a campaign of what seemed to him good
processes in the lives of the individuals who owed him
the most. The first man was a dealer in secondhand furni-
ture. He started sending people to the storekeeper, asking them to take his card with them. The second debtor
was a farmer. He made arrangements for the men to sell
eggs direct to friends in the city. The third was a music
teacher. To him he sent pupils. He explained that he was
doing all he could to help his debtors pay him. In
about a year the money was collected.

You invest your money well only when you invest
your life better. He who will not compromise himself is
less likely to waste his sustenance. The danger in seeking for riches lies in the temptation to ego satisfactions
in luxury at the expense of the fulfillments of our capacities. When you cooperate with good fortune, she re-
sponds. When you aid life, she aids you.

45   The Habit of Success

It is often better to fail at the wrong task. If you
weren't blessed with the ability to fumble, society
would have made you a permanent slave. Laugh with
joy and gratitude, then, when you can't go on doing
the wrong thing, no matter what it is.

Whenever you see a lackadaisical young man who
seems to have no ambition and no energy, do not de-

cide he necessarily is weak. How weary you yourself have felt when confronted by tasks for which you were unsuited! Boredom is a warning that a person cannot safely continue the type of life he is living.

This is fine theory, you tell me, but man must work to eat and eat to live. Granted, and in a pseudo civilization I'd add, that little concern for a man's fitness to work is ever given. He is put into an army as gun fodder, or into the ranks of labor, without regard to his nature. If he fails, it's just too bad. That is the old attitude and the present practice.

Whoever employs you does so for a selfish motive. You must be worth more to him than the money he pays you. The more you are a live, dynamic, alert, efficient being, the more likely you are to secure work. When seeking a job, ask yourself: "Do I want employment more than I want my own way of life? Can I under present conditions have both?" It's first of all a question of adaptation.

There are two types of people: workers and those who think they want work. The workers toil to make themselves indispensable; those who merely want work want it on their own terms. This does not deny the social injustice in relation to work, but defines only one's personal classification in view of the economic limitations.

There are cases in which the problem is exceptionally difficult, not because of self-indulgence or laziness, but from special talent. And yet, no matter how unusual or unique a man is, he still must decide whether he wishes work, or self-expression. If he asks security, he must seek it wherever and however security is found, adjusting his outer conduct to economic necessity, while keeping his beliefs and inner integrity. I can pile bricks for eight hours a day and toil for social betterment as many evenings as I choose. I can work and still think. I do not need to become regressive because the world is, or as greedy as the money changers.

And however progressive I may be, there is no need to collide with society if I choose fields of effort where my difference does not operate. Good luck is first of all a matter of effective organization of one's personality in relation to the world as the world now is.

The secret of solving most unemployment problems is made up of four parts:

1. Adjusting to the social era in which you live.

2. Refusal of compromise: that is, keeping your inner attitudes and beliefs and striving constantly to strengthen them.

3. Putting all you have into whatever work you do, making yourself so valuable that the world *needs* your services.

4. Having avocational, or nonearning, outlets, not only to accommodate your restless, creative powers, but gradually to help bring about better social and economic conditions to fulfill those powers.

People fail when they do not maintain a balance between these phases of effort; fail most by underdoing or overdoing adaptation. As long as compromise is excused as inevitable in the face of social usage, its deforming influence will continue. Cursed by spiritual anemia, its victims will continue to shamble about as zeros in the universe.

Norbert Wales has long been confused and uncertain about his future. He does not know what to do. Everyone talks about "this good chance" and "that opening," but Norbert doubts. He has failed too often to have much faith in anything. There are a few certainties, however: the young man likes to talk, he loves people; it amuses him to gad about; regular hours are difficult; change and variety seem essential. His father scolds him because he will not stick to routine.

Norbert consulted a vocational guidance counselor, who suggested organizing his likes and dislikes into a mental program, a concept of a way of life to which Norbert might successfully adjust.

"Let's see," the expert mused, "you won't stick to routine, but like to argue endlessly. There is a hint here that you wish to convince others and are inclined to propaganda. You love the excitement and variety of meeting all manner of people. Now, let's picture that you contrive to do this professionally, wouldn't it be good fun?"

"Sure, but I've got to earn a living."

"Any less fun if you talked for some purpose?" pursued the consultant.

"Why no. More chance, I'd say, to conquer in the discussion."

"Good. Now, you like to persuade, you like to educate others, you like to carry on a cause or crusade. Ever think of selling life insurance?"

"No, I never did."

"Well, let's think about it. It's a compatible use of your temperamental twists. Why not picture what your days would be like if you took up this work. Continue your picturing every night for a while, to help you see if this work isn't a means of having the running about and the talking you love to do."

There are three types of vocational problems: that of the young person still in school, who wishes to prepare himself for the right work; that of those whose schooling is past, but who still do not know what they want to do; and that of the mature individual like Norbert Wales, who at one time had "gone into bookkeeping" because it offered a living.

The adjustment principle holds for all three situations: namely, suiting the task to the man and not the man to the task. In fact it is the only permanently successful procedure.

In nearly every university these days there are means available for determining your abilities. The department of psychology in your nearest college will tell you how you can be tested.

Write a biography of the way you wish your next ten years to go. You cannot, of course, make the future come to pass merely by wanting it. But there is magic in wanting. Somehow, knowing what you want, defining your purposes, seems to start a chain reaction. Write the story, not only of what you wish, but of how you intend to overcome some of the odds of destiny.

One thing is certain. No man or woman ever failed in life, or even in social achievement, who persistently followed his interests, sharpened his wits, taught himself to concentrate and pushed his avocation, if a vocation had not been found. Get ready to win and you will not lose.

Suppose you were on your deathbed, looking at life as if you were through with it, asking: "If I could live it over again, what would be important?" Whatever is significant at the time of death is equally so now.

As soon as possible, purchase the little book called *On Vital Reserves,* written by William James. Read it ten times. Study especially what he has to say of the second wind in effort. Then practice the habit of keeping on when your first wind fails until the second one comes.

The following evaluator is not offered as a vocational guide, but as an example of systematic thinking:

100%—Genius
90%—Strong plus
80%—Strong
70%—Strong minus
60%—Average plus

50%—Average
40%—Average minus
30%—Weak plus
20%—Weak
10%—Weak minus
0%—Void

Record your idea of your percentage of endowment or interest on the following scale, then unite the main endowments into one ability.

Vocational trends for preference analysis:

Mathematical	....%	*Place here the five strongest*
Medical	....%	*endowments*
Political	....%	
Military	....%	Example:
Social	....%	Brown might fill it in as follows
Mechanical	....%	
Chemical	....%	Dramatic 90%
Electrical	....%	Literary 80%
Religious	....%	Psychological 80%
Educational	....%	Artistic 70%
Commercial	....%	Critical 90%
Literary	....%	
Poetic	....%	His ability total was: Dra-
Artistic	....%	matic critic—82%
Architectural	....%	
Scientific	....%	
Legal	....%	
Musical	....%	
Agricultural	....%	
Dramatic	....%	
Domestic	....%	
Psychological	....%	
Critical	....%	
Manual	....%	

This is merely a condensed example of vocational balancing. There are over five hundred general vocations and several thousand special variations. The twenty-four above are only vocational trends.

46 *Accept Your Mistakes*

Did you ever notice that people troubled by remorse do nothing to pay life back the debt they owe? They continue to act as destroyers. They will do this as long as our ethics justifies predatory emotionalism.

By this I mean that remorse makes people melancholy, heavy, negative. It destroys their usefulness and hinders their power to cooperate. As such it is wholly evil. When its gloom is ego satisfaction, when its sorrow is masochism, it has no excuse for being.

Learn, therefore, to accept mistakes. They happen. That is the edict of the new compassion. It brings miracles to pass.

Four years ago, Clara Atwater seldom smiled. Sorrow brooded in her eyes. A cohort of sins followed her about, pricking her conscience with their javelins. Their uproar so confused her she made mistakes constantly.

That way lies madness and increasing failure. Dread of failure makes more failure. Guilt makes us guilty. Belief in trouble as punishment destroys all courage and all power.

One thing is certain; you can't correct mistakes if you feel ashamed of having made them. Those who secretly believe themselves deified are chagrined when something goes wrong. Being saints, and utterly wise, their conduct should of course be perfect. The rest of us know how easy it is to be at fault. We're making mistakes all the time—and patiently correcting them.

Hell is in your memories. The cauldron of remorse for what you did not dare to do is worse than any pain from wrong efforts. A forthright striving, whatever its outcome, gives one protection by its very strength.

A present trouble is bad enough, why load it with past woes? Yet you always do this the moment you let yourself become morose about your problems. Some people carry the weight of five decades on their backs and blame each new day for the load. He who wastes his time doubting his own impulses carelessly gathers the bitter fruit of his dilemmas.

Here is a list of some of the mistakes we make most often:

Twelve Mistakes to Avoid Making

We don't stop to see what we want.

We fear to declare our purposes.

We act hurriedly, not stopping to "feel" our way.

We take no action: not daring to go ahead at all.

We take fright from the first little mistake, as if it were serious.

We worry because of ignorance of all the facts.

We become emotional, personal, self-involved.

We are confused by the delusions of duty.

We exaggerate the difficulties, out of fear that they are too great.

We distort the present out of all perspective.

We focus on the troubles instead of on their conquest.

We miss the delight of the adventure—the adventure of overcoming.

Mistakes are essential to success. No man ever achieved anything worthwhile who didn't make scores of slips. *A perfect score is the ideal of a perfect ass.* If you don't dare to challenge a situation, it will challenge you. Never let a trouble get in the first blow. Take a chance when action is important. To fail to move is worse than thoughtlessness. There is such a thing as thinking too long and too much. This is particularly true in human relations. *He who hesitates is bossed.*

The secret lies in action. Think if you can, but act anyway. After all, if you never make a mistake, you can't correct it. You obey the law of averages when you wish to win in the long contest of life. He who is up when luck is with him, down when fortune stoops, soon becomes dizzy from the bumping. Hold back your ardor when the game is easy. Save it for the times of struggle. On your balance does your success depend.

When ashamed of your imperfect score in the service of unselfishness, you are likely to fall into circular brooding, lying glumly on your bed thinking about your troubles, but never stopping to analyze a single fact long enough to understand it. We learn from past mistakes only when we keep confidence in the one who made them. If you were the doer of the wrong deeds, you won't learn better as long as you blush at your imperfections. Once you are bitten by the flea of self-abasement, you follow his example, crawling under the soiled garments of convention.

Under this degradation of self, it is easy enough to disparage everyone else. We transfer our inferiority to our intimates, a mistake that may curse us forever, unless we learn to give it up. Never make others feel guilty by what you do or say. Watch this, for everyone likes to pass blame along, putting uneasiness in someone else's heart.

This, in a sense, is a key mistake, an ignorant habit that lies under scores of our common failings. Note how it underlies this list:

Seventy-two Ways to Make Sure of Failure

Coercing others

Making people feel guilty

Passing the buck

Trying to exploit people

Brusque assertiveness

Not giving people time to present a point

Shouting to convince

Finding fault with half-expressed ideas

Being unwilling to cooperate

Putting too great a burden on intimates

Speaking slightingly of ideas

Losing track of what you were saying

Thinking people are usually willful

Judging people by externals

Treating your children disrespectfully

Fretting until people obstruct you

Choosing the wrong moment to mention something

Assuming too much responsibility

Being too final and arbitrary

Frightening others by pressure

Having a rigid sense of justice

Treating a trouble as permanent

Sanctifying your prejudices

Trying to live vicariously

Seeking a scapegoat

Supposing childbearing saves a marriage

Blaming a man for his heritage

Being a "halfway" man

Being afraid to experiment

Losing the adventure drive

Focusing on consequences

Yielding to discouragement

Thinking poor work will pass

Depending on your luck

Having no alternatives

Developing no plan

Enduring situations too long

Trading on blood relations

Treating people from a money standard

Thinking your marriage partner a "possession"

Not being courteous to intimates

Becoming angry in arguments

Patronizing associates

Trying to impress others

Expecting understanding without explaining

Being condescending to women

Being motherly to a man

Infecting children with your fears

Retaliating for hurts

Being proud and secretive

Taking advice without reasoning

Being too literal, merely logical

Not keeping a sense of humor

Upsetting by bluster

Not knowing when to retreat

Trying to cover all points

Failing to concentrate your forces

Setting your heart on certain outcomes

Thinking man is civilized

Believing in our conventions and standards

Expecting ideals to be realized

Judging life by how it now appears

Believing in the finality of fate

Not taking chances when action is imperative

Not daring to shake a situation up

Letting things go until a crisis

Not keeping to a central aim

Not watching the trends

Resisting what has happened

Not looking around corners

Counting chickens before they're hatched

Letting the first few failures upset you

To read this list of common failings is only of value if you and I check on our own special delinquencies, or get our wives to tell us which they are—*and then do something about them.* Most people, when they realize they have made a slip, become egotistic and offended about the predicament in which they have placed themselves. They act as if it were the other person's stupidity which created the situation. When in such a mood, they do not give an associate a chance to see why the situation must be cleared up. He who keeps his hurt pride out of the picture, and at the same time writes down fully all the pros and cons of a matter, soon wins cooperation for a change of plans.

List the reasons why you made a mistake and compare them with the better action. The facts, if they are there, speak for themselves. In any case, give up your fear and anger; they do no one any good.

This is, in a sense, the very basis for successful handling of difficulties, for the first step in conquering them is always to yield your resistance because you have them to conquer. Most people make the mistake of focusing on the trouble instead of on overcoming it. Ask yourself: "What is this trouble for? Has it come just to nag me, or did I need it for my growth or understanding?" You seldom get what you don't deserve.

To convince yourself of this fact, figure up what past troubles did for you. Ask yourself if you would be willing to be without the growth they brought to you, then see if you won't grow from your present painful situations. It is well, in fact, to remember all the points in the following list:

Ten Ways to Deal with Trouble

Never resist the arrival of trouble. Bothers come about every so often for almost everyone.

Be kind to all who cause a quandary. A tender reception softens the hardest blow.

Become familiar with a problem as rapidly as possible. Familiarity breeds insight.

Try to discover what you needed to learn from a bothersome experience.

We grow through pain as well as joy. Many dilemmas are never overcome, but outgrown.

Try to see how interesting and romantic your situation is, yes, even entertaining.

Ask yourself if you are really as upset as you think you are.

Try to find the humorous side of the predicament. It is always there.

Always try to get the people and things that brought your difficulty to help you.

No matter what happens, remember that good nature is usually invincible.

There is only one effective way to deal with a crisis: meet it squarely, head-on. Any other way involves compromise—and compromise, like evasion or expediency, is the essence of defeat. A cataclysm cannot be averted by turning your back on it.

A good many years ago a crisis confronted a group of men. One of them, knowing that firmness is power, cried out: "If we don't hang together, we'll hang separately." Patrick Henry understood the law of decision. Years later, a captain was asked to surrender his ship. His eye was on the wind. Instead of giving up the battle, he swung to the enemy frigate's stern and raked her from a safe position. John Paul Jones knew the importance of sudden, firm decision after adequate deliberation.

History records hundreds of such victories, swift actions with all the power and boldness of men thrown into crisis situations. It is still popularly believed that such masterly decision comes from spontaneous bravery. Research shows this is not so. Failure results from thoughtless daring quite as often as does success. The hero is not impulsive. *He prepares.* Goethe defined genius as "an infinite capacity for taking pains." I doubt the greatness of any casual victory. One doesn't win often by mere chance.

Was Hannibal less brave because he invaded Italy

through the back door of the Pyrenees, taking the Romans by surprise? His crossing of the Alps with full equipment and elephants is one of the remarkable feats of history—but Hannibal's imaginative planning, his timing, his decisiveness, did nothing to minimize his stature as a hero.

In a world now dominated by technology, we need to gain a new respect for that greatest of machines—man's brain. We must renew our faith in his capacities and see how they may be trained for the further conquering of circumstance.

Did you ever ask yourself what skill is? You are injured in a motor accident. A woman from a passing car comes to your aid. Tenderly and swiftly she bandages your wounds. She is a nurse. She began serving you when she taught her fingers and steadied her nerves, giving her power to care for injured people. Her unselfish act depended upon the development of herself. So, too, when you recognize, strengthen and use your memory; when you release, quicken and clarify your imagination; when you find, improve and use your judgment, you are being yourself, preparing yourself for service.

Such altruism is not self-sacrifice. It is self-use. That noble phrase: "He who loseth his life shall find it," does not mean a supine throwing of your powers into the gutter. Virtue is not in goodness, but in the power to fulfill that goodness. Nothing that is weak continues to serve. You cannot be kind and insipid.

The art of living, then, consists in keeping your vigor: in discovering how to direct it, a task we are long in learning. The lesson begins in infancy when with lusty lungs we cry for our desires. Sensation, that first factor of awareness, is telling us we are hungry, cold or wet. We want comfort. The self, conscious of help from parents, nurses, family, utters its demands. This is right and as it should be up to or until we are able to perform for ourselves. Then must the ego adjust itself to the wants of other egos and the long lesson has begun.

This adjustment of the self to the world is a matter of evolution, of gradual awareness. Like a child in a tantrum, we become dominating little egotists unless we discover that happiness necessitates skill in finding what measure of freedom is possible to us all, and among us all, in the furtherance of our aims.

A Few Rules for Meeting a Crisis

Stop to think, then dare to act. Make yourself an instrument of conquest.

Your wits were given to you for just one purpose: to use. The greatest secret in all life can be put in one sentence: *Learn to listen to your mind.* Cast aside all interfering biases and think—without the drags of yesterday. Intelligence lies in new ideas about present facts: in seeing, hearing, touching, calculating about them.

How often we believe that if this or that were only changed, we could accomplish miracles. And it is true. If this or that personal idiosyncrasy were only given up, if some morbid egotism were cast from us, success would come. Meeting a crisis starts within the self.

Warnings are many to open minds. To a literalist, a whistle is a whistle, a boom a boom. His mind is closed to their meaning. He fails from being practically impractical, so efficient in many things he can't read their significance.

Millions ask for guidance. It is all about them. Everything is full of signs that egotism never sees. The secret is simple. Shed your pride as you would a pair of outgrown spectacles. Modern science grinds better lenses than those of convention or conceit. And that's a point thousands of our bilious young cynics need to remember. There's such a thing as knowing so much one doesn't know anything—about the essential art of living.

Adjustment requires contact with reality. You must not only see life, but look into it. That is why he who is concerned only with things never commands them. The biggest fool is he who knows the facts but doesn't know what they mean.

He who seeks the portents directs the outcomes. It isn't in the facts alone that truth lies, but in the tendencies, trends, motions and evolutions of those facts. Life is never still. Yesterday has changed into today. Motives are at work moving things along. Success depends upon how you react to this dynamic flow.

The ancients counseled us to think before acting. Today we add: feel before you think. Intellect without emotion is empty of power. You can speculate for years on countless theories without caring for any of them. He who succeeds must first long to do it. Passion is the energizer of purpose.

Without purpose people are dead, or might just as well be. There are too many aimless intellects cluttering the way of progress. Don't stop among them. Feel again, feel about anything. There is no motion without emotion. Action and passion are really one and the same.

What enrages you about your situation? Choose some point that irritates your soul. Decide to attack at that place. But teach yourself that sturdy calm which comes from mature passion. An infantile temper strikes and splutters, shouts and contends. Like a quarreling boy, it depends upon threats and noise. Well-developed rage is still; still as death. It feels no impulse to quarrel. It calculates. It has little to say. It looks for something to do. Don't abuse your anger, use it. Guide it with judgment and teach it wisdom. But listen, listen to its voice, for temper knows where to close in and how to take hold.

Every man has a hero and a coward in his breast. He can identify himself with either. One is known by the company he keeps, loved for the things he hates. Turn your anger against your cowardice and courage will follow.

In any case, don't emulate a corpse. Having heard about silent, strong men, some people draw into a stony grandeur, inhibiting their feelings with an icy chill. Quiet effort and unobtrusive achievement do not deny gaiety and a smile.

The pose some people put on of hours of deep, dull deliberation, the ponderous way of giant contemplation, is sheer fake. The pseudo genius goes through his silent antics to make himself believe he is intelligent. Judgment, when true, is swift as light. Jove threw thunderbolts and played with lightning. Turn your hours into seconds. A sodden sage is senile.

Limber your body to nimble your wits. The more serious your problem, the more you need to move. Never sit and brood. Get up. Walk about. Stretch your arms. Fill up the wind bag a few times. When a car goes up hill, it needs more gas. When thinking is hard, you need more blood in your brain. Good reasoning is a matter of mechanics. Don't forget, therefore, that the fool lies still and thinks he thinks. Your wits work when you do.

In other words, act as if you had some brains. If you follow the ways of confident men, people will place you in their category.

This doesn't mean that you have to rush about with the crowd. Millions keep on the move but with the aimlessness of baboons. You can't jiggle your way to wisdom. Mere action and lost motion are synonymous.

Act, therefore, only to a deliberate end. Get something started, then watch it. As soon as it is moving, life gives it creative power. You help yourself by helping it. Start something and give it your attention. Act "as if" you were solving your problem.

You get somewhere also by shedding your Pilgrim's load of gunk.

Twelve Causes of Failure

Belief that money is an absolute, so one can't afford to act.

Collision between the past and the present, contradictory conclusions, letting your dead grandfather spoil your life.

Stopping from the confusion of opposing policies.

Weak acceptance of sickness as an absolute.

Delusion that situations are unchangeable.

Habit of yielding when the "hard place" arrives.

Conflict of ideals from divergent values.

Collision of pleasure and achievement principles.

Stalemate from basic incompatibility in intimacy.

Stress from opposite direction of growth in a human relationship you developed this way—she that.

Stagnation from injurious environments wrongly accepted.

Blockage from fear and moral anxiety.

Never allow an impasse to remain twenty-four hours without doing something to start it changing.

Eight False Premises and How They Work

Supposing things and situations are as important to others as to you.

Thinking others will suffer as much as you do in certain difficulties.

Imagining destiny and the world as against you—that there are "schemes" involved.

Believing there is no way out, no answer.

Picturing yourself or the other person as having no ego rights and preferences.

Placing yourself at the center of the universe, either as great or little.

Accepting the world as civilized instead of veneered with a masquerade of manners.

Holding that the truth is known and right and wrong are absolute, instead of relative.

Twelve Troublemaking Notions

Believing the world owes you a living.
Thinking there is an easy way to make money.
Refusing to form a work habit, a real work habit.
Keeping yourself too tired from play.
Thinking you can't learn how to sleep soundly.
Blaming others for your constant difficulties.
Supposing that luck is against you.
Waiting for good times to come before trying.
Caring more for comfort than for conquest.
Letting other people rule your life.
Carrying burdens that belong to others.
Letting the lure of love destroy your reason.

Some Acts Miscalled Selfish

To select your own vocation.
To choose your marriage partner.
To make your own friends.
To determine your beliefs.
To find your best environment.
To use your own time.
To have your normal recreation.
To protect your privacy.
To decide your own responsibilities.
To measure your own standards.
To define right and wrong for yourself.
To refuse all dishonest compromise.

It does no good, of course, to read these lists unless you discover in them the points that touch your life and then do something to change the situation you are in. In any case, you can at least localize troubles and keep them from dominating your life. You can, if you will. You can, if you stop to think about them. You can, if you plan a score of ways to accomplish the needed changes and choose the methods that seem suitable. Even if you didn't act soon enough to avoid your troubles, there is some action you can still take. Remember, *each new day gives you another chance.*

What to Do When Your Forethought Comes Afterward

Be willing to admit you made a mistake.

Realize that no one is infallible.

Consider what you would have done had forethought come in time.

Balance what has happened against what you still can do.

Make an adjusted plan of what can be done to repair the situation.

Do it—execute your plan as efficiently as possible.

Don't expect the perfect result you might have achieved.

Accept the need of more endurance and patience than would have been originally required.

Don't blame destiny for your own past hesitation.

Vow to keep on until you gradually correct the whole difficulty.

Eight Ways to Win Through

Keep your attention on the present.

Do all you can with the problem now.

Let the results be what they may.

Keep impersonal toward all trouble.

Listen for a guiding "hunch."

Expect your wits to work.

Use your five senses; watch.

Act, keep the initiative always.

Twelve Good Points for Bad Troubles

The stranger your problem, the more unusual must your solution be.

Extreme difficulties call for radical measures.

Don't believe your trouble is great until you prove it so.

Problems in life, like those of arithmetic, require calculation.

Find both the something and the somebody most responsible.

Don't assume that those who caused your difficulty were always willful, or even had you in mind.

Don't blame others for unintended hurts.

Don't fail to condemn bad conduct just because you won't accuse the person who did it.

Face the facts of a problem no matter to whom they point.

Remember that angels don't live in your neighborhood, nor in your family. We are all human.

Treat a sick body and a sick mind with the same mercy.

Most troubles are caused by ignorance and misunderstanding. Remove both before you proceed further.

The Secret of Problem Solving

Make every aspect of your problem your familiar. Put yourself into each part of it as if you were in it physically. See, hear, touch everything you think about, make your thought utterly visual, fully tactile, and dramatize the conversation.

Now trace the relations between the parts you have thus made real. See how one part or person affects each other part or person.

Start a free association, a free floating movement of memory material in relation to each of the more important points. Then try a reasoned memory recall, a controlled or logical association to get the guidance of past experience.

Organize this material into groups and systematize it.

Experimentally formulate some conclusions and compare them. You are likely to find your answer.

The important thing, then, is not to fool ourselves into the belief that nothing will go wrong in the future. We must be ready to cope with our difficulties of tomorrow, and do a better job of it than we did today.

There is one basic principle in the handling of all troubles which is seldom understood, namely: *do not focus for more than a few minutes on a difficulty before you look to see how you can change the whole situation.* This is the way a physician handles sickness, how surgery deals with an injury, how engineering meets mechanical weaknesses. There is not frenzied focus on the event, but a forthright act such as calling an ambulance, giving medicine, building a buttress, putting in some struts.

Next to this great principle of objective science is that of accepting experience and of keeping an impersonal perspective upon it. You go to the theater, read novels and adventure stories and sit spellbound at a travelogue just to listen to the drama of other people's troubles.

Never make a decision without alternatives. Never turn to alternatives until you must. Lay them out and have them ready like money in the bank.

Practice in handling trouble is what makes you wise. You learn to solve problems by dealing with them, not by running away. Nor do you help yourself, or anyone else, by complaining about your sorrows. *An active mind, a busy hand and a shut mouth accomplish miracles.* Think up a series of moves and then analyze them. Tear them to pieces. If you uncover their weaknesses first, no one else will.

That reminds me of my *ninepin technique*. I'm convinced people can solve their problems more easily if they think up at least nine possible answers and then try to knock them down by rolling criticisms at them, just the way we roll balls in a bowling alley. I choose the solution that stands the hardest knocks and still remains upright. And I crack a lot more problems that way because I find that what often seemed to be the least significant suggestion turns out to be the best solution.

Truth in general is like the sky; it spreads over a situation, but never moves a mountain. One iota of practical wisdom has more power than all the philosophies. When dealing with trouble, then, we must be concrete, asking ourselves: "What is wrong? Why did it happen? How can we right it?" This is the order of wisdom.

"When shall we begin? Where shall we start? Who can help us?" This is the way of common sense. You get what you want only by knowing what you want, and by having a sliding scale between it and what you can get. Move up your wants as fast as circumstance yields. What you can have at any particular moment is a relative matter. It depends upon your concentration, insight, skill and persistence in the face of a constantly changing situation.

The important thing is not to know a few useful methods, but to form the habit of orderly thinking. Do you want contentment, for example? Then make a balance sheet to help you.

THE SATISFIER-ANNOYER BALANCE SHEET

In every situation there are things that please you and things that irritate you. Your response to them is quite personal and rightly so. The things that you like, someone else might dislike. That is his affair. In most cases, there is enough for you and enough for him. Discover and select

your satisfiers. Help them to increase. Avoid and discard
your annoyers. Don't let them destroy your happiness. You
may like privacy, and your husband prefer people. Let him
have the people, but tell him they can't come into your privacy.

REPEATED CONTACTS

The more times you do a thing, the easier it is to do.
The more contacts you make with the things you fear in a
troubled situation, the less you will fear them.

Select some points that disturb you, that you feel you can
deal with most easily. Make repeated contact with them.
Keep on doing this. Gradually deepen and broaden your
contacts to include difficult points. In this way, you can overcome the severest odds.

DEBUNKING OPINIONS

Most everyone's thinking is colored by a mass of stupidity gathered from the unthinking influence of other people.
Everyone delights in pouring nonsense into the ears of anyone in trouble. It's a relief to get rid of the gunk that makes
us suffer, so we vent it when anyone asks us what we
think.

To free yourself of such psychic poisons, separate all of
your own carefully thought-out ideas about a situation from
the nonsense of others. But don't follow your own ideas
unless you have checked out some of them by actual tests.

REALIZATION

Haziness, headiness and hooey make up half of humanity's headaches. Theory without any tangible basis in reality
lets millions become tangled up.

Stop every so often to realize where you are going, what
you are doing and who is getting you to act like a sick
baboon. The simple act of taking stock is a rare act indeed, but one that is essential to intelligent living.

THE SOCRATIC METHOD

The old Greek philosopher was a bore, but not as some are who visit at your house from morn to midnight. Socrates bored into people's statements to see what they were made of. He tried the same questioning process on his own ideas.

About thirty percent of the things you think you think are as you think you think them; the other seventy have quite a different emotional basis. Your desires and true beliefs have a way of playing blindman's buff. You must corner the inner facts, or you and everyone else will be fooled.

WRITING IT DOWN

Maybe you are a genius, in which case this suggestion is unnecessary. But if you aren't one of the great minds of the century, it is better not to try to think your problems out in your head, and especially never to think about any problem after 10:00 P.M.

Write down all the facts you know in a rough-and-tumble manner. Just jot them down. Then put them in some sort of order, the unimportant facts on one side, for example, the significant ones on the other. Having done this, restate your trouble as you imagine five widely different people would describe it, and let your selection include someone you don't like, or who doesn't approve of you. Then work on your problem with all these new attitudes in mind and with the facts down in black and white.

ASSEMBLING THE FACTS

More than half of the time the mistaken handling of troubles comes from not knowing the facts well enough to act. Form the habit of listing all the points you know, then list the points you aren't sure of, and figure out how you could discover the needed facts. Begin your effort by getting the needed information. When you know sixty percent of what

is needed, go ahead. The rest will come as your effort progresses.

Get More Facts

It is strange how few people remember that we have
libraries in America and that in those libraries are encyclopedias, volumes of reference, dictionaries, geographies, textbooks, charts and all sorts of other helps to "reality thinking."

Years ago, three men decided to seek homesites in a distant state. The first man took the first train there and back.
He returned, disappointed, having spent $285. The second
man wandered all summer through several states, confused
and uncertain. The third man went to the library and read
geographies, encyclopedias, studied maps, weather reports,
agricultural statements. He sent to the state for data. He
learned more in a few days than the other men could discover in years of hunting. The inquiry cost $1.87. I know,
for I was the third man.

Free Association

The best of every man's thinking is inspirational. His intellect may not be so great an instrument, but a gathering
of ideas is valuable indeed.

Four of the commonest mistakes made in the face of trouble are:

1. Impulsive, thoughtless action.
2. Following intuitive, unchecked "hunches."
3. Carrying out logical but inadequate ideas.
4. Fear of any action at all.

Invite your intuitive impressions. Allow your "hunches"
to come up. Then think about them, quietly and logically.
That is sane meditation.

Paired Comparisons

People make the mistake of thinking all over a problem in
a confused and disorderly way. A girl, for example, is try-

ing to see which of her men friends she likes the best, and why. Does she compare them systematically, judging Henry's imagination in contrast to John's creative fancy? Not at all. She thinks vaguely about them both.

When in trouble and not sure which way to turn, list the points that are alike in each course of action and compare them. Then count up your *fors* and your *againsts* in order to come to a decision.

THE FINE ART OF DISCARDING

Most of the time, we carry too much baggage on the journey of life, hold onto things we no longer need. When in trouble, reduce everything to the lowest common denominator. See what values you could give up, what efforts are no longer important, and even in what ways you can reduce your estimate of your difficulty to a smaller measure. I know a woman who thought she was very unhappy because she wasn't married. When she discarded the idea that she was "an old maid" and saw what the marriages of some of her friends were like, her trouble disappeared.

THE ACTIVE FACTOR

In every situation there is one thing or one person or one circumstance that started the trouble and kept it going. This is the active factor. It is always the most important thing to find. If you can discover it and checkmate it, you have the problem in hand.

The active factor in war is usually economic greed. If that could be recognized and dealt with firmly, there would be no war. It isn't the hates of peoples, it's their stupidities and laziness that let a trouble grow.

THE SEVEN-STEP THINKING PLAN

There is a really important series of steps one should follow in thinking about any trouble:

First: Consider and assemble the effects, or facts, in the situation.

Second: Seek the causes or forces that created the effects.

Third: Try to discover the principles, the general basis of the particular problem.

Fourth: Record and consider all the people in the dilemma.

Fifth: List the places and the things concerned with the matter.

Sixth: Designate the most important influence in the dilemma, person or thing.

Seventh: Decide at what time something should be done about it.

THE ADJUSTMENT VALUE

There are no perfect answers, no complete solutions, no great gains without some losses, no goods without some evils, no winning without some failing. You can't always do right. It isn't humanly possible. You can only do what is the best: an adjustment value of rights and wrongs. Sometimes you must deliberately do a small wrong to avoid a greater one, or select a minor evil to achieve a major good. It is better to hoodwink your father and marry the man you love than not to marry him from fear of duplicity.

GETTING MORE OUT OF LIFE

Most people think about life and their troubles in a compromised way because they try to see all the odds and evens at once. You can't do that successfully. Lay out your wants on one piece of paper. Put your limitations on another. Don't modify either list. Make them explicit. Then on a third paper, put the balance point: how many of your wants you think you can get this season, after considering your liabilities. Plan to raise your balance point every year.

DYNAMIC BORROWING

Most of the time, it is foolish to do things yourself, with your own hands, feet, efforts and speech. The modern method is to use a device to work for you. You don't scratch the dirt in your garden; you use a plow. Use some similar instrument to accomplish your more personal ends.

Once upon a time, the nephew of a certain wealthy man went to the Middle West to live. "Borrow money every so often and pay it back the day it is due," the uncle advised. "Why?" asked the nephew. "To let people know you are honest. If you don't, they may never discover it."

THE PHILOSOPHY OF "AS IF"

The way you behave affects the way you feel and the way you think. Your reason was given you to plan your behavior; your power of purpose is made to carry the program out. If you act like an ass, you will soon feel like one. A calm manner and firm conduct are contagious. You soon begin to think with poise and execute with courage. Make a personality program of the way you intend to act in trouble. Then stick to it. And remember that if you "pretend" that something you want *is* true, it may well *become* true. That, as Havelock Ellis pointed out in *The Dance of Life,* is the practical significance of fiction in human life. That also is what Hans Vaihinger meant in his great book *The Philosophy of "As If."*

LET ANGER DESTROY FEAR

When fear upsets you in dealing with difficulties, seek for some points in the trouble that anger you. Dwell on them until your rage is aroused. The fear will disappear. Or try wondering about a trouble. Release your curiosity. Fear will diminish. I know of a girl who was once romantically upset over a worthless man. She lost all her sexual love for him as soon as she began to be curious as to what he was really like. A dominant emotion always obliterates a lesser one.

THE POWER OF CHANGE

Everything and everyone is in transition. It is possible that your husband won't be half as stupid in another twenty years. He is maturing—gradually. The problem to settle is not whether you can endure him now, but whether there is hope of his improvement. Don't compare what he is with what you want him to be. That will drive you crazy. Study his rate of change. This measurement of transition is the only way to estimate anything.

DIAMONDS AND DIRT

In South Africa, they dig for diamonds. Tons of earth are moved to find a little pebble not as large as a little finger-nail. The miners are looking for the diamonds, not the dirt. They are willing to lift all the dirt in order to find the jewels. In daily life, people forget this principle and become pessimists because there is more dirt than diamonds. When trouble comes, don't be frightened by the negatives. Look for the positives and dig them out. They are so valuable it doesn't matter if you have to handle tons of dirt.

PLAYING WITH COMBINATIONS

When you have no light on a problem, deliberately select a series of opposites to each important point. Then combine one opposite with another and see what happens. This method always wakes up your wits. For example, I once wanted to be a portrait painter, but I also wanted to eat. I combined "sausages," then "spats," then "folderol," "garret," "groans," with "painting portraits." The combination gave me mental colic. I decided I didn't want to spend my time wearing spats and doing folderol to paint the wives of sausage manufacturers, who would let me groan in a garret while I painted.

NEVER STOP TESTING

Humanity owes to its experimenters all the most important progress that has been made for centuries. You and I know this. We now and then remember it halfheartedly. In the face of trouble, however, we seldom keep a wise, safe and careful experimentation at work. We become peeved and petulant instead.

Keep testing, and move pieces of the situation about. Try out this and that person's response. It's amazing how things fit when active fingers move the picture puzzle of trouble about.

ASK FOR HELP

I know a stock broker who has made a fortune, not from his work in Wall Street, but from a simple technique that requires only some postage stamps, some paper and envelopes, and some time. Every day of his life this man sends out a batch of letters asking people for help of one kind or another. Not all the people know him, nor does he know all the people he writes to, but his batting average of response is so high that people are always doing things for him (and he for them, by the way). Five letters a day was his quota. I got two such letters, and what he wanted me to do seemed so easy and reasonable that I did it. Later, when I met him, I asked him how he happened to write to me. He explained his simple secret, and now—with his blessings—I pass it on to you. Obviously, his method works, because with my help he got a book published which became a best seller. And other people have helped him in other ways. What makes his recipe foolproof is that it is not one-sided. He's always ready to help you, *if you ask for his help*. Living proof of the wisdom of the Bible: *Ask and it shall be given*.

49   *A New Bill of Rights*

When madness is about us everywhere, it becomes important to formulate some protective conclusions. Look, if you will, at what is happening around you. In your home some member of your family takes a stand strongly opposed to yours as to how to live in a group. It is possible that you believe in a few basic human rights that should not be surrendered by any self-respecting person. Your aunt, or some other relative, pays not the least regard to your privacy and trespasses continually on your personality.

Or maybe you dislike the freedom of the young. You claim a respect for your seniority which your children do not accord. If you are of the old school, you expect to tramp into your daughter's room, no matter what her age. She is "your child," isn't she, you say. Home life today is a hodgepodge of conflicting views on the rights and privileges of people.

The same mad contrasts appear in the body politic, and while they are less evident in America than in Europe, rampant forces are asserting their brand of liberty, or planning their species of domination. Trade unionists go to as predatory extremes as the industrialists ever used.

A few—a pitiful few of us—plead for intelligent solutions and a middle course between ruthless riot and rigid regulation. Extremes only destroy. Free government in the nation is impossible unless we keep it in the family. It has to be a spirit before it becomes a fact. Communism in the home makes anybody's property everybody's property, permitting the group to prey upon the individual. Fascism in the home permits everybody's property to become that of a single overlord —the greediest and most ruthless person there. It allows personality to prey upon the group.

Democracy—seldom yet practiced in any land, and rarer still in any home—gives individual rights in relation to group rights, fulfilling personal needs without destroying social requirements.

Such were the convictions of our forefathers. They are borne out by the researchers of modern science. Biologists, anthropologists, sociologists, psychologists, know and realize the importance of the health and vigor of the individual not only to himself but also to the society which is but a multiplication of selves like his own.

You cannot with conviction and energy meet all your daily problems without some insight into the basic rights of every man. You cannot know as fully as you need to know why constructive selfishness is necessary to a wise unselfishness, why the sacrifice of any individual (which means you) is as destructive to the welfare of society as it is injurious to your own happiness.

As long as our forefathers believed it was evil to be clean, medicine was forced some centuries ago to challenge the applications of unselfishness rooted in the ethics of that day. The first doctors were hounded into dark cellars, there to do their work. Today, the integrity of the mind and its rights is being fought out. We believe in the sanctity of man's biological rights. We know his instinctive and dynamic urgings are essential to life. We see that upon his right of choice his very manhood depends.

HOW MODERN SCIENCE CLASSIFIES AND DEFINES GOOD
SELFISHNESS

As a biological urge—for the preservation of the species.

As an automatic expression to protect the organism.

As a functional process to carry out the natural actions.

As an instinctive response to fulfill the individual powers.

As an emotional drive to protect personal integrity.

As a striving to further primary purposes.

As a cerebral energy to strengthen initiative.

As a subliminal uprush to emphasize spiritual intent.

As an athropological impulse, to differentiate the ways of
man.

As an identity sense to guard the social unit against submergence.

Put in everyday speech, such a list means that you
have the right to a private place or sanctum of your
own: a room, haunt, retreat, or camp, that will act as
your shell; that you may be and remain an uncompro-
mised personality. Food, clothing and shelter are basic
privileges, and to this end social orientation and the
protection of others are essential. Because of this, liberty, fraternity, equality become vital attributes of mutual aid, and without them there is no security, no
rest, no play, no reward for effort.

Thus it is that in human contacts love, sex and freedom are the goal of effort and the personal "shell"
becomes the family castle, so revered by every English-
man as "his."

Some examples of *good selfishness* and what it is:

To believe that what is best for you won't in the end hurt
others.

To believe your only duty is to do the best you can.

To allow yourself time to think, to decide, to develop.

To protect and foster your inherited abilities.

To go always and forever with your love.

Never to stop growing, expanding, evolving.

To respect your own nature and accept it as a trust.

To protect yourself against all compromises and defilement.

To love your neighbor *as* yourself, and know what *as* means.

To marry only because you love, no matter who suffers.

To believe that the right of choice is always yours.

To refuse all sentimental external shibboleths.

To defy and ignore all evil forms of selfishness.

To carry on against the entrenched stereotypes.

To refuse the coercion of evil unselfishness.

To be yourself—utterly, honestly, always.

Our present political liberties depend upon the Magna Charta, without which we Americans would never have had a Constitution for our national protection. Today we need another Magna Charta: a personal Bill of Rights to protect selfhood. Such an instrument should include:

The right to refuse coercion as a means of determining conduct.

The right to develop one's beliefs of good and bad, free of conventional pressure.

The right to a constructive expression of every facet of personality.

The right to develop without regard to "rules" so long as society is not injured.

The right to be judged by all one is and does in a decade rather than by a single action.

The right to put full responsibility on one's ancestors for all questions of character type.

The right to grow "after one's kind," self-expansion.

The right to environment after one's need: suitability.

The right to eat according to one's constitution.

The right to work according to one's endowment.

The right to rest and to repair one's organism.

The right to joy: to play and recreate one's vigor.
The right to space, for air and action.
The right of freedom, for experimental living.
The right to love, and the fulfillments of sex.
The right to obey the instinct of race preservation.
The right to nurture, give protection to the young.
The right to shelter from natural dangers.
The right to protect and warm the body.
The right to avoid injury and sickness where possible.
The right to drink, the quenching of thirst.
The right to wash, and the fulfillment of self-respect.
The right to all bodily functions in privacy.
The right to think and feel according to one's conviction.

It should be evident in considering these modern interpretations of the art of living that constructive selfishness does not consist in egotistic self-advancement. There is no anarchy in the new philosophy. Nor is consideration of others denied. You do not, to be sure, yield to their self-indulgent demands, or fear to let them suffer when they seek your submergence, but there is no predatory greed in the application of the new teachings.

Your self-concern is for the end of protecting and fostering your abilities, that you may continue to grow. Believing that what is best for you is, ultimately, best for the other person also. You allow yourself time to think, to decide, to develop. You seek the larger ends and the broader services, and from a respect for your own nature, you protect yourself against others. You love your neighbor as yourself, remembering that Jesus thus advocates self-love in no uncertain terms.

Following His example, you also refuse sentimental shibboleths and deny all ignorant forms of selfishness, carrying a sword against the entrenched conventions. Refusing all the coercions of evil unselfishness, you marry only for love, no matter who suffers, determining to be yourself, even in intimacy.

You also realize that any neglect, misuse, or denial of your powers leads to such a weakening of your personality that you must in the end become a taker from life instead of a giver to life: that is, acting upon evil selfishness.

One of the difficulties between primordial greed and constructive selfishness lies in the attitude of the liberated person, who believes that he has a right to ask others to consider his personality quite as much as he is asked to consider theirs. He does not expect to be indulged, or to be able to act destructively without unpleasant consequences.

If I trespass upon others, I must thereafter be so nervously on guard against their retaliation that I cannot again bask in the sun of nonchalance.

It might even be better for the world to lose the benefit of a few men's great gifts than that their predatory behavior should be socially excused and followed. It is natural that we should seek recognition, but to debase others for this end, or to exploit them for our advancement, is ruthless.

Nor is predatory behavior less evil because in the name of commerce it is so common. It is easy to make selfish acts seem virtuous and to turn blame upon crusades for a better life, finding a scapegoat and condemning someone else for our sins. Nor are such self-seekers willing to receive only what they earn; they demand that every constructive act pay interest for centuries. If they do you a service, they expect to live on it for a lifetime. You see this in women whose womb toiled in lieu of personal effort, who wish to be enthroned thereby forever.

Whenever possessiveness or jealousy, domination or

vainglory, rules in human conduct, it is greed, not constructive selfishness, that is in control. The egotist demands the right of way. His urge is insatiable. Utterness is the measure of his wants. He does as he pleases. He wishes you to do as he pleases. He may be careless, you must be meticulous. Inanimate objects come in for condemnation, when they resist him. Golf clubs are broken if the ball is missed, objects which refuse to work are kicked. Nor are these scavengers of compliance willing to win the worth they demand. It must be yielded to them.

The greedy are skillful at hiding their intent; no others are so adroit at concealing their purposes. They it is who talk the most about lovingness and virtue. Some examples of *evil selfishness*:

To prate of "self-sacrifice" while remaining possessive.
To "deny yourself" and talk about it endlessly.
To "do good" and tell everyone about it.
To think of anyone's duty to you.
To live vicariously on the world or others.
To take more from life than you give to it.
To advocate democracy, but live on the poor.
To believe in class position and the right to luxury.
To pray to God for any special consideration.
To wish to win in any competition for personal exaltation.
To consider your pride in matters of truth.
To refuse to believe in mutal aid.
To seek personal gain without being socially useful.
To substitute predatory actions for cooperation.
To refuse good actions because of self-protection.
To work for money without regard to service.
To think of yourself with pride.
To refuse surrender of your ego to cosmic law.

The contrast between the purposive content of good and evil selfishness is even more enlightening:

Impelling Forces in Evil Selfishness	*Impelling Forces in Good Selfishness*
Fear, anger, disgust	Caution, courage
Sex lust, subjection	Elation, wonder
Parental dominance	Tenderness, nurture
Acquisition, flight	Curiosity, sex love
Repulsion, pugnacity	Gregariousness
Self-assertion, pride	Cooperation
Embittered self-abasement	Compassion
Jealousy, hate, envy, greed	Construction, manipulation
Revenge, dominance	Play, reverence, love
Vanity, intolerance	Self-preservation, honor
Egotism, vindictiveness	Respect, tolerance
Possessiveness, power-seeking	Independence, mutual aid
Anarchy and autocracy	Democracy and freedom

It must be evident that from the newer attitude modern philosophers believe that suffering serves a definite end in that it teaches us that greed, envy, jealousy, revenge, hate and duplicity must be given up. Pain punishes us until we learn to discard evil self-seeking and pseudo unselfishness for constructive self-concern and comradeship.

The expansion of consciousness is the greatest means by which this evolution comes to pass. We do not overcome our primitive conduct. We outgrow it. Antagonism, hostility, become inactive when we see how foolish they are. Impatience and meanness disappear. Haughtiness and stubbornness change as self-will is regenerated into a spiritual awareness of self-hood.

For this reason, wise people do not attack or try to force predatory natures into goodness. They know it is a matter of development. They decide whether or not a person is still a barbarian. If so, talking will do no good. Balance up your contacts with a greedy man.

If you must remain in his society, consider your essential needs. Formulate your purposes into definite convictions, planning at least six unyielding courses of action. Then carry out your purposes, quietly, firmly, resistlessly, without further debate. *Waste no time justifying your plans to an egotist.*

Silence is equally wise when selfishness is the result of conflict between the different sides of our natures. Part of us wants to be angelic while another attribute is full of mischief. The devil in us has his way sometimes, and then a strange, sad self appears that looks at the moon with mellow longing, remorseful for its fury.

There isn't much gain after all when the virtuous sides of us come into dominance unless we have a clear idea of what generosity is. Too many people swing from greed to garrulous goodness, giving to others for display.

You know the type of man who has no sense of the organization of life, who takes off his shirt for you. He seems loving to a fault. His ways are charming. But wait. In the end, you or someone must pay for that shirt. He'll have nothing of his own by and by and will need yours.

Some examples of *evil unselfishness* and what it is:

To do good for the sake of self-glory.

To watch and ward anyone else's moral conduct.

To give to the poor, while living on them as a parasite.

To belong to a humanitarian society for the sake of belonging.

To establish great foundations with stolen money.

To sacrifice the good of society for the comfort of your children.

To glut your ego with the greediness of mother and father love.

To refuse to allow others to experience the consequences of action.

To refuse others growth through pain when necessary.

To sustain any church or institution in which you don't believe.

To overwork or die for the comfort or pleasure of anyone.

To do an act "against life" to please anyone.

To deny yourself and become an ultimate burden.

To repress others by an egotistical saintliness.

To hold to any custom, creed or dogma against the social good.

To worship God as an act of social propaganda.

Study the average unselfish person and you will discover he is a contracting personality, who takes life out of others by his spiritual emptiness. His is a mock goodness, the virtue of omission. He has inhibited his impulses, repressed his desires and dwarfed his mind in the name of holiness. He is shocked that you believe in dynamic living. He fears your advocacy of vigor, your respect for nature's powers. He tries with all his might to restrain you, restrict you, shrink your ardor. He hates your enthusiasm, which word, as you may know, means "God within."

The worst form of unselfishness is the fear of self. It is strange that mankind did not see long ago that such an attitude leads to sickness and death; the principle is so clear in nature. Every living thing that rejects its powers becomes diseased. Its success depends on how and where it grows, on the direction of its creative power. At no point is inhibition, suppression or constriction a constructive process.

It is for this reason that contracting personalities end in failure and unselfish people become burdens upon their fellows. The life story of every self-sacrificer proves that in the end he sacrifices everyone, including himself.

He sickens and must be nursed. He fails and must be carried. He becomes a destroyer.

Expanding personalities, on the other hand, do not take from others by their quickening magnetism. They win the competence upon which the dependent feed. By using themselves instead of sacrificing themselves, they become the instruments of growth and security. Advocates of the old unselfishness love the heroic acts of self-denial. It is the splurge of martyrdom they seek, one large enough to satisfy their vanity. They seldom bother to do the little acts, the minor tasks, the daily dozen duties. If they do, you are told about it forever.

Contrast this unseemly egotism with a brief history of some of the attributes of *good unselfishness*:

To do unto life what is constructive in life.

To do unto others as you would be done by if you were they.

To surrender the self to every understanding of truth.

To obey constructive nonresistance, overcoming evil with good.

Never to sacrifice the best interest of mankind for your family.

To give yourself wholly and creatively to your life tasks.

To give yourself to the crusade of eliminating competition from work.

Never to hesitate to perform any true social service.

To obey and to advance the spirit of cooperation.

To hold to and obey the doctrine of mutual aid.

To be as willing to live for others as to die for them.

Never to live on a personal income without serving.

To refuse every privilege of class, caste and position.

To live on a basis of democracy as well as to preach it.

To allow even children privacy, liberty, equality and free thought.

To permit every human being the right of choice.

Never to pray to God for any special privilege.

In a nutshell, your bill of rights is to refuse all compromises of yourself, if, and only if, you refuse ruthless ego satisfactions as well. Without cooperation, individuality has no rights; without integrity, mutual aid has no power; without a union of such love and wisdom, no service remains.

50   *Your Place in Life*

Life may begin at forty. It depends on what you mean by life. Death begins there much of the time. Suppose you are a woman just past this once "fatal age," when our grandmothers put on lace caps. Suppose your children are married and living at a distance, your husband has died and left you his insurance. Your past has not led to the discovery of abilities, your nerves are torpid, your glands sluggish, you face financial uncertainty.

Is life beginning with nonchalance? If not, what is the answer to advancing age? It lies in three acts:

1. Retrospection
2. Introspection
3. Prospection

At the best period in your life, what interested you the most? Did you love the great outdoors? Then go to it now. Exercise, build up, carry the vigor of youth into age. Did you love art, music, mechanics? Did you dream of travel? Follow these aims, even if you have to take your journeys in an atlas, or make music on a mouth organ. Resurgence is a law of life.

Following this survey of the past, make an analysis of the present. Look into your heart. What longings endure? Dare to pursue them. Eliminate every day one or two things that cause discontent. Find two or three acts that give you satisfaction. Keep shifting steadily toward an agreeable way of life.

Lastly, calculate on the future. What sort of fun do you crave for your old age? Ripe fruit is richer, sweeter, more red-cheeked than when it's green. So, too, with life. The later days are the mellow ones, if you decide to make them so.

The change that came to Mrs. Medford is characteristic of what has happened in many lives. It came from a shock. She stopped off on the way back from California to see her Aunt Susan. Sue was living with her daughter, Patty. She had become one of those whining dependents, who have no life of their own and take what little their children grudgingly give. Sue, at fifty-six, was an old woman with desperate eyes and nothing to do.

"I'll never become a senile dependent," Mrs. Medford vowed to herself, "never, never, never! I'll begin now seeing to it that every year of my life I have more friends, more interests, more action. I'll live so vitally I won't need to dread loneliness."

The way to meet old age is to grow in youth and middle life. Only he who has learned to make each moment yield what that moment possesses has an answer to experience. He may finger a flower, looking into its face, or hold a purring kitten in his lap. If he cannot gain what those stray touches of reality have for him, he cannot receive ecstasy from the kiss of a goddess or the accomplishment of heroes.

The greatest honor and the rarest love become prisons unless we live in and beyond the exceptional glory. Nor is there any way through the routine of business and a dull home to the gladness we have lost, unless we strive for joy in any setting and with all our energy.

The way out of a wrong job, or through a wearisome marriage, is in the finding of such nourishment in the unfortunate situation that the spirit is fed to win a better destiny. Sullen rebellion and supine surrender bring no satisfaction. Embittered people, as well as the patient ones, are put upon by fate.

If there is no immediate solution to a problem, just keep looking for one. Life cannot be met save by initiative. You improve what you once begin. To believe that "about all one can do is to bear it" is no answer. Those with pious resignation are more unfortunate. If I serenely fold my hands and wait—until someone gets me out of my difficulties—I'll wait forever.

Trouble seeks all who forsake dynamic living. As long as men thought the plague to be the will of God, it was the will of God. When they ceased to fold their hands, they ceased to be plagued.

The answer to the pressure of our days is one and simple: *daring*. Dare to live while life is passing; you'll never live otherwise. Set a limit on what you are willing to bear. Call this your adjustment margin, your wall of personality. "They shall not pass" beyond that line, no matter who or what they are. Regardless of the trial, the duty, the burden, drop it or them when they attempt to intrude upon your spirit.

Have your times of looking at the clouds, or hearing music, or fiddling with machinery, or laughing with "your kind of friends." Go where they are who feed your soul. Don't die of psychic malnutrition. Involved in the duties and details of your day, you merely exist, with rare escapes into drugging excitement. Millions in

America work and run: work to live, and run to forget; drinking cocktails or petting madly in the moonlight for an hour's oblivion.

The greatest need of every man is an inner purpose, a belief or endeavor he carries about with him in his heart. This establishes a sanctum in the center of consciousness to which he returns for strength.

Such a holy place lay in the depths of every great painter, composer and poet. We find it in the scientist and engineer. They lived in their subjective depths, producing new ways of life, seeing new reasons for striving. If faith in the orientations of consciousness and the power to attain finer and wiser ways of living flow from this inner dynamic, the individual continually renews himself, reshaping his days and finding strength to go on with the task of living. It is this creative insight that millions lack.

You won't find it, however, if you don't first find yourself; nor your place in life without a sanctum in your spirit. No matter how much adaptation you must make, don't give up an inner sense of being. In it is a power that you can use for adjustment. Day by day, year by year, more of what you seek will then find its way into your pattern of opportunity.

Adjustment is made by yourself and in yourself. It springs like Hercules from his mother's womb from the moment you dare to say once and for always: "I shall never compromise myself." It comes permanently when you put by forever all ego satisfactions, all envious, ruthless and infantile retaliations, all jealousy and greed, seeking the art of selfishness in the spirit of science as an obedience to nature.

Such a creative unfolding as this leads to the miracle of discovering your identity. There follows a rejuvenation of the forces of the basic character, a real breaking out of the tomb of egotism, a momentum of unfolding into an ever-increasing life. It is as if the old individual, with his struggles, his resistance and bewilderment, were suddenly gone. So dramatic is the moment that those who have known it never can forget.

Many have compared this change to religious conversion. The significant fact is that the person who experiences this for the first time sees life as it is; and as he touches reality, he is also able to reach back to the core of his consciousness. He will never again be separated from life or from himself. He no longer thinks or acts from old values, but rather from a new spiritual awareness. Life stretches ahead as an adventure of which he is no longer afraid.

Handy Guides to Help You Become the Person You Really want to Be!

_____ BIORHYTHM, Arbie Dale, Ph.D.
80779/$1.75

_____ BODY LANGUAGE, Julius Fast
80388/$1.75

_____ DREAMS ARE YOUR TRUEST FRIENDS, Joseph Katz, Ph.D.
80734/$1.75

_____ est: 4 DAYS TO MAKE YOUR LIFE WORK, William Greene
80600/$1.95

_____ FACE LANGUAGE, Robert L. Whiteside
80033/$1.50

_____ HOW TO LIVE WITH ANOTHER PERSON, David Viscott, M.D.
80272/$1.95

_____ META-TALK, G. Nierenberg and H. Calero
78879/$1.50

_____ STAND UP! SPEAK OUT! TALK BACK!, Robert Alberti, Ph.D. &
Michael Emmons, Ph.D. 80641/$1.95

_____ UP FROM DEPRESSION, Leonard Cammer, M.D.   HP
80631/$1.95

Available at bookstores everywhere, or order direct from the publisher.

POCKET BOOKS

POCKET BOOKS
Department RK
1230 Avenue of the Americas
New York, N.Y. 10020

Please send me the books I have checked above. I am
enclosing $_____ (please add 35¢ to cover postage and
handling). Send check or money order—no cash or C.O.D.'s
please.

NAME_____

ADDRESS_____

CITY_____STATE/ZIP_____

HAROLD ROBBINS

25,000 People a Day Buy His Novels.

Are *You* One of Them?

_____ 81150 THE CARPETBAGGERS $2.50

_____ 81151 THE BETSY $2.50

_____ 81152 THE PIRATE $2.50

_____ 81142 THE DREAM MERCHANTS $2.50

_____ 81153 THE ADVENTURERS $2.50

_____ 81154 WHERE LOVE HAS GONE $2.50

_____ 81155 A STONE FOR DANNY FISHER $2.50

_____ 81156 NEVER LOVE A STRANGER $2.50

_____ 81157 79 PARK AVENUE $2.50

_____ 81158 THE INHERITORS $2.50

Available at bookstores everywhere, or order direct from the publisher.

POCKET BOOKS
Department RK
1230 Avenue of the Americas
New York, N.Y. 10020

Please send me the books I have checked above. I am enclosing $_____ (please add 35¢ to cover postage and handling). Send check or money order—no cash or C.O.D.'s please.

NAME_____

ADDRESS_____

CITY_____STATE/ZIP_____

POCKET BOOKS

Carlos Castaneda

With TALES OF POWER now available in a Pocket Book edition, one of the most popular authors of the twentieth century completes his journey into sorcery.

"We are incredibly fortunate to have Carlos Castaneda's books..."
—The New York Times Book Review

_____	80676	TALES OF POWER	$1.95
_____	80498	THE TEACHINGS OF DON JUAN	$1.95
_____	80424	JOURNEY TO IXTLAN	$1.95
_____	80497	A SEPARATE REALITY	$1.95

Available at bookstores everywhere, or order direct from the publisher.

POCKET BOOKS
Department RK
1230 Avenue of the Americas
New York, N.Y. 10020

Please send me the books I have checked above. I am enclosing $_____ (please add 35¢ to cover postage and handling). Send check or money order—no cash or C.O.D.'s please.

NAME_____

ADDRESS_____

CITY_____ STATE/ZIP_____

POCKET BOOKS